INSIGHT *Pocket* GUIDES

Baja
Peninsula

Quiniela 14

MEXICO

APA PUBLICATIONS

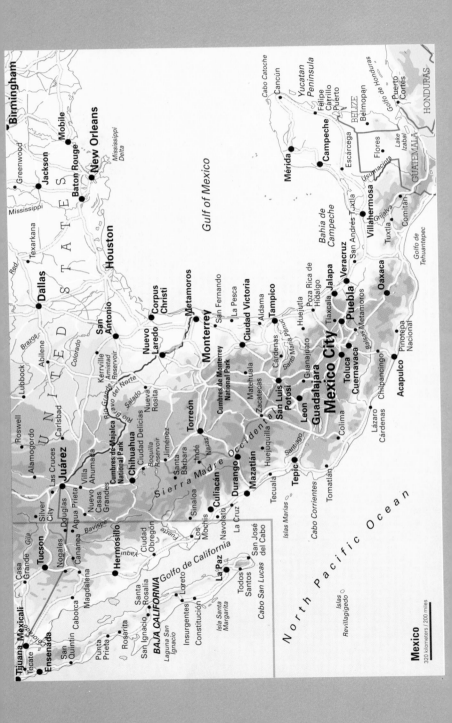

Mexico

320 kilometers / 200 miles

Dear Visitor!

Baja California is only a few hours' drive away from Southern California, but apart from the busy border towns it remains largely unexplored and uncommercialized. In the Jesuit interior, often just a few miles from the main highway, are bare mountains and the remains of deserted missions.

It is this very inaccessibility which is making the Baja peninsula increasingly attractive to adventurous travelers, who set off in dune buggies or four-wheel-drive vehicles to negotiate the narrow, rugged trails once familiar only to pedestrians and mules. Hundreds of miles of coastline are accessible only by sea, although Baja's reputation as a sports-fishing paradise is leading to the creation of connecting roads. Insight Guides' correspondent has planned a series of itineraries which help you discover the best of Baja, while avoiding both the pitfalls and the potholes. The tours begin at brassy Tijuana, where most people cross into Mexico, and take you right down the highway to the southernmost tip, with optional detours to other border towns, little fishing villages, deserted Jesuit missions, and to a lagoon where gray whales breed.

 John Wilcock is a freelance travel writer who has contributed to several Insight Guides on Mexico and America's West Coast. He traveled through Baja by bus, and was captivated by the combination of barren desert and idyllic bays, of sleepy villages and glitzy new tourist developments. In the following pages he shares with you the discoveries he made in a land which is quite unlike the average tourist destination.

Hans Höfer
Publisher, Insight Guides

C O N T E N T S

Pages 2/3:
View from the Old
Mill Hotel

Pages 8/9:
Nuestra Señora
de Loreto mission

The narrow Baja peninsula which stretches 1290km (800 miles) south from the California border originated about 4 million years ago when the peninsula separated from the Mexican mainland. With most of its 140,000sq km (54,000sq miles) composed of mountains and desert peninsula, much of which receives less than 25cm (10in) of rainfall a year, it can hardly have seemed the most attractive of regions to Hernán Cortés and the other Spaniards who came across from the Mexican mainland.

Cortés, drawn to La Paz in 1535 by reports of black pearls from the rich oyster beds and spurred on by rumors of a land whose golden mountains were guarded by a tribe of black Amazon women led by the beautiful Queen Calafia, stayed for only one year and it was another 60 years before the arrival of Sebastian Vizcaíno, who received a friendly welcome from the Indians.

Usually in Spain's conquest of the New World the sword came first, followed by the missionaries. In Baja's case, however, the Jesuit order (founded by Ignatius Loyola in 1534) began petitioning for the right to 'civilize' this new land almost from the year of its discovery and indeed, after some unsuccessful attempts at military occupation, it was decided to relinquish Baja to the ecclesiastical authorities. Nevertheless, it was 1683 before the first Jesuits arrived in Baja to propagate the Christian faith: hostility from the indigenous people and the sheer aridity of this barren land had frustrated all of Spain's earlier military expeditions.

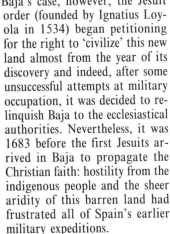

Accompanied on their initial expedition by 100 soldiers under the command of Admiral Isidoro Antondo y Antillon, the Jesuit fathers made a smooth landing at La Paz, led by the versatile

Queen Calafia

Painting displayed in La Paz library depicts Cortés landing in Baja

Father Eusebio Kino, astronomer, cartographer, navigator and even something of a doctor. Next day, Kino wrote, they were awakened by 'a great horde of savages, painted and plumed, waving their bows and arrows with threatening gestures ordering that we depart.' Failing to placate the Indians, the Spaniards withdrew.

Next year, 1684, the admiral returned to the peninsula, again with Kino, this time landing on October 6 at a point about 49km (30 miles) north of today's Loreto and 10km (6 miles) from the Indian village of Londo. It was the day of St Bruno and they named the port after the saint. For two months the expedition dug trenches undisturbed and created a camp.

The Jesuits learned enough Cochimi to give short sermons and teach the catechism to kneeling children, who in turn taught their parents, but the admiral felt the place was sterile and unhealthy – there had been but one slight rainfall in 18 months – and wanted to leave. So 'because he did not find a way to live in the port of San Bruno,' observed Fray Francisco Javier Clavigera, '(he) embarked with his missionaries and all his people and returned to New Spain.' It is from the books of Clavigera that we owe much of our knowledge of the early history of New Spain (Mexico).

Of the ill-fated second Baja expedition, nothing remains at San Bruno today but some weathered stones. It had been a wasted three years which had cost the Crown almost a quarter of a million pesos. The Jesuits, however, were not so easily discouraged. They sought souls, not land or gold. Kino, an inspirational leader, yearned to expand his parish and eventually he persuaded the Royal Council of the Indies that the religious zeal of the Jesuits could conquer where the army had failed.

Kino's partner was to be Milanese-born Juan María Salvatierra, born in Milan in 1648, who was now Visitor General of the Missions. He had joined the Jesuits when he was 20 years old, volunteering

11

This painting of Salvatierra and his flock can be seen in La Paz library

for work overseas, and his enthusiasm had been ignited by Kino, who nevertheless remained behind in Sonora when the landing at what is now Loreto was made on October 19, 1697. The missionaries dug a trench around a tent they had designated as a chapel and deposited in it an image of the Virgin Nuestra Señora de Loreto which they had carried in procession from the boat. Despite some Indian hostility and occasional attacks, the Loreto mission flourished and was completed in 1704, by which date there were 70 permanent colonists and 200 baptized Cochimi Indians, after a number of the fathers had learned the Cochimi language in order to teach them the faith.

Salvatierra was at Loreto for 20 years, overseeing other missions during his two-year stint as Padre Provincial and mastering a dozen languages, both native and European. In 1699, Salvatierra's assistant Padre Francisco Piccolo built a road through the mountains to found the Mission of San Francisco Xavier de Vigge-Biaundo, which was subsequently taken over by Padre Juan de Ugarte, another impressive figure who had successfully raised funds for the society from private sources after the Crown had lost interest, and who had now learned the Cochimi language. To finance the Loreto expedition, Salvatierra and Ugarte had literally walked the streets of Mexico City appealing for funds.

Back in his native Honduras, Ugarte had been a teacher of philosophy but now, at 41, he was clearing land, building dams and an irrigation system (traces of it remain today), planting corn, figs, dates, grapes and cotton. He hired a weaver to come and teach the Indians how to make garments and he also established a school and built a hospital.

Much of the opposition to the early missionaries came not from the ordinary Indians but from their self-appointed medicine men, or *guamas*, who wore capes of human hair. The religious fathers, by uncovering their tricks and robbing them of their prestige (wrote the Jesuit historian Peter Masten Dunne) became the immediate enemies of the *guamas* who 'played skilfully on the credulity of the people' forming a close caste in which they initiated the most astute among the young braves with secret rites. and 'pretended to inflict sickness and misfortune as well as heal and care.'

Sixty-five kilometers (40 miles) across the mountains northeast of Loreto in the middle of the peninsula are three small missions sharing the name Commondú, built between 1714 and 1737. To the northwest is another mission, La Purísima, built in 1717, which eventually, under Padre Nicolás Tamaral, became the most populous of the missions, with 2,000 residents. Father Tamaral, later to be murdered by dissidents, described the Indians as being tall and robust with dark chestnut-colored skins and beards, and hair extending well below their shoulders.

In 1720, Ugarte sailed down the coast to found a mission at La Paz, while another one, Guadalupe, was being built at Guasinapi in the mountains above Mulegé, where Ugarte had found the hardwood timber for building a boat with which he scouted sites for new missions. Two years later, a plague of locusts wiped out almost all the crops and the mission's supply of corn could only ensure the survival of a few. Many Indians ate locusts for lack of anything else and it was this diet that killed them.

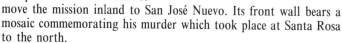

After a visit from the new Procurator, Father José de Echeverria, it was decided that the time had arrived to spread the faith in the south. Padre Tamaral built the first of two new missions – now known as San José Viejo – but a plague of mosquitoes caused him to

Indian revolt

move the mission inland to San José Nuevo. Its front wall bears a mosaic commemorating his murder which took place at Santa Rosa to the north.

Eventually the Indians' discontent, fanned by the *guamas* who saw their influence being superseded by that of the Jesuits, erupted in open rebellion in 1734, when a group of malcontents incited their fellow tribesmen to burn the southern missions, along with the handful of soldiers and some of the missionaries who were unable to escape. For a while, the fathers gathered at Loreto but once the rebellion was extinguished they returned to their missions at the entreaty of those Indians who had not joined the uprising. A presidio was built at San José del Cabo and garrisons installed there and at the other missions.

In 1767 Santa María, the last of the Jesuit missions in California, was constructed north of El Crucero, near the coast. Because it was the most northerly of the Baja missions, Santa María became a major staging point for supplies when the missionaries extended their sway in Upper California.

The following year, Father Junípero Serra, along with 13 other Franciscan friars, arrived at Loreto to take over from the Jesuits who, after 70 years of hard, pioneering work, were being dramatically expelled from the New World, the consequence of a row in Spain between their order and the nobility, whom they had accused of corruption. The expulsion came without warning and the unfortunate fathers were required to depart immediately without their possessions. All 16 of them – eight German, six Spanish, two Mexican – were guarded and treated almost like criminals on their journey back through Mexico. Several of them fell sick and died on the way. Along with them went 36-year-old Father Clavigera, an instructor in the Jesuit college at Guadalajara, who subsequently settled in Bologna to write his four-volume history of Mexico, published in 1780. In 1786 he completed a *History of (Lower) California,* which was published after his death.

He wrote, of course, about a race that was still extant. Epidemics of smallpox, dysentery and other European diseases, together with a catastrophic rebellion and barren years in which the pitahaya and other desert fruits failed to mature, had reduced the Indian population by about 75 percent before the end of the 18th century.

In May 1769, Captain Gaspar de Portola, commander of Spanish forces in California, met up with Father Junípero Serra at the Santa María mission, outfitting two ships, the *Santa María* and the *San Carlos,* to head north and explore the new territory. Serra, who had successfully converted many Indians in central Mexico, suggested that as there weren't many Indians left in Baja and the land

San José del Cabo mission

La Paz in the 19th century

was so arid, two religious orders were unnecessary. It was agreed that the Dominicans would administer the missions in Baja and the Franciscans those in Alta California. Thus, on May 12, 1773, 18 Dominicans arrived at Loreto and fanned out to the various missions. Father Vicente Mora arrived to take charge of the Dominicans; he was accompanied by Padre Luis Sales, and it was the latter who best chronicled the following years.

Sales, deputed to find a position for a northern mission, settled in 1788 on a site on what is now the free road between Tijuana and Ensenada, 65km (40 miles) south of the border in the valley of La Misión, from which he opened a road north to join up with the mission at San Diego. In 1793, records show a congregation of 171 Indians, but by the end of the century only 5,000 of Baja's Indians remained.

By the time Governor Manuel Micheltorena ordered that the lands surrounding the missions be given to the Indians, few were left to receive them and the 1849 California Gold Rush siphoned off many of the rest. Today, the only remaining Indians are a handful of Kilihuas in the northern reaches of the San Pedro Mártir mountain range. The entire population of rural Baja is less than one person per square mile.

In 1821, a decade after the revolution on the mainland, the Mexican Republic was created, having won independence from Spain, but it was three more years before Baja became a separate federal territory with its own governor. In 1847, during the Mexican-American war, US troops briefly captured La Paz and around this time a handful of adventurers, such as the maverick William Walker in 1853–4, unsuccessfully tried to annex Baja. Although President Polk's suggestion that the US ought to buy Baja for $5 million dollars was never acted upon, the *Norteamericanos* got a strong foothold anyway when Mexican president Porfirio Díaz granted vast concessions to foreign investors, hoping to speed up Baja's development. The Hartford Company of Connecticut paid $16 million to develop all of Baja Norte, planning a railroad from the border to San Quintín with ports there and at Ensenada. When no rain came they sold out to an English syndicate who sowed vast areas of wheat, and built houses and mills, but also waited fruitlessly for rain. A French company developed copper mines at Santa Rosalia, which in 1953 were taken over by the

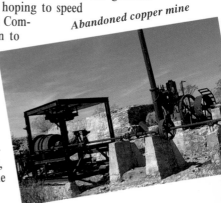

Abandoned copper mine

Traditional homestead in the Museum of Anthropology, La Paz

Mexican government, and on the island of San Marcos the Kaiser Corporation operated a gypsum plant. With the help of foreign investment, Carmen and San José islands in the gulf harvested extensive salt deposits and a salt works at Guerrero Negro is said to be the largest of its kind in the world. The Valley of Mexicali, farmed by the Colorado River Land Company, was turned into a vast agricultural region. In the late 1930s much of this land was sold to Mexican farmers,who formed communities known as *ejidos*.

In 1911, while revolutionaries led by Francisco Madero were sweeping the 30-year Porfirio Díaz dictatorship from office, an anarchist named Ricardo Flores Magón (born in Oaxaca, in 1873) gained support in Baja for a movement that sought a more fundamental revolutionary shake-up, which he saw as part of a worldwide revolution. Although subsequently disowned by mainstream socialist movements as far too hot-headed and radical, he has been dubbed 'the Great Precursor' of the revolution.

Prohibition in the US understandably turned the border towns into havens of booze, sex and gambling in the years between the two world wars – a situation that persisted in part until relatively recent times. But although the Mexican border cities still lure millions of Californians, and increasing numbers are venturing further south, the region's current prosperity stems as much from traffic going in the other direction, and from the revenue generated by the thousands of foreign-owned industrial plants which operate south of the border.

Welcome to Baja

Historical Highlights

1535 Hernán Cortés leads an expedition to La Paz seeking pearls, stays only one year.

1542 Portuguese navigator Juan Rodríguez Cabrillo crossing from the mainland to explore the Baja coastline, heads north to his death in the Channel Islands.

1587 Sir Thomas Cavendish intercepts the Spanish galleon *Santa Ana* off Cabo San Lucas and steals its treasure.

1596 Sebastian Vizcaíno meets friendly Indians on a visit to La Paz.

1615 Captain Juan de Iturbi secures a concession from the Viceroy of New Spain (Mexico) for pearl fishing. One of his two ships captured off the cabo by the Dutch.

1683 An expedition to Baja, accompanied by Jesuit Padre Eusebio Francisco Kino, arrives in La Paz, builds both a church and a small presidio but eventually returns to the mainland.

1697 Padre Juan María Salvatierra succeeds in establishing a mission at Loreto, which is completed over the next five years. Loreto becomes capital of Baja California.

1699 Padre Francisco Piccolo builds a road through the mountains to found the Mission of San Francisco Xavier about 20 miles southeast of Loreto.

1711 Death of Padre Kino, who is said to have baptized almost 5,000 Indians.

1720 Father Ugarte founds a mission at La Paz.

1722–3 Plague of locusts causes widespread starvation.

1734 Indian rebellion, which is quickly extinguished.

1767 The last of the Jesuit missions constructed near El Crucero.

1768 Jesuits are expelled from the California territory.

1773 Dominicans take over all the Baja missions.

1821 Mexico gains independence, and the republic is created.

1824 Baja California becomes a separate federal territory, with its own governor.

1828 While trapping beaver in the desert, the first known American visitors barely escape dying of thirst. A storm levels Loreto, and La Paz becomes the new capital.

1847 Baja occupied by American forces during Mexican-American war but returned to Mexican ownership under 1848 peace treaty.

1853 American adventurer William Walker sails into La Paz to proclaim Baja a separate republic, then retreats back to the US.

1875 Comprehensive maritime charts of Baja coastline completed.

1911 Dictatorship of Mexican president Porfirio Díaz comes to an end. Anarchist Ricardo Flores Magón briefly gains support for a revolution in Baja.

1930s Land in Mexicali Valley sold to farmers who form communities called *ejidos*.

1945 Treaty signed between US and Mexico concerning water from the Colorado River.

1951 Northern Baja becomes Mexico's 29th state.

1953 Mexican government takes over the French copper mining interests in Santa Rosalia.

1970 Whales come under formal protection of the law.

1994 Signing of the NAFTA (North American Free Trade Alliance) between the US and Mexico.

1994 Assassination in Tijuana of Luis Donaldo Colosio while campaigning as the PRI (Partido Revolucionario Institucional) candidate for the presidency.

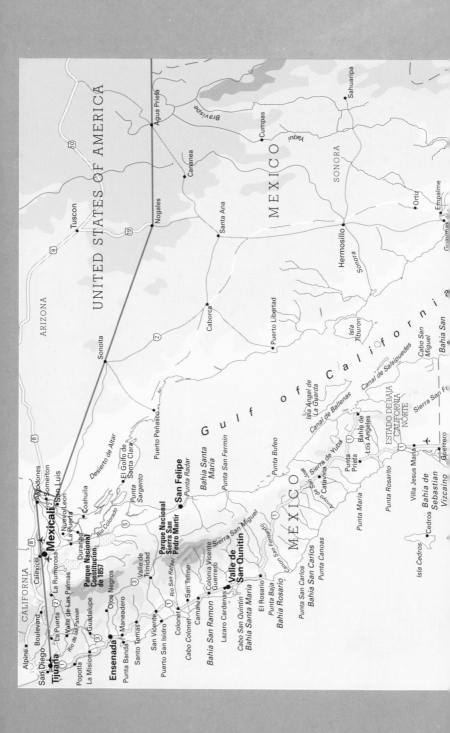

The Baja Peninsula

100 kilometers / 62 miles

Day Itineraries

1. Tijuana to San Quintín

You will probably cross the border at Tijuana, and this route leads you due south through Ensenada. Routes to and from the other border crossings, Tecate and Mexicali, and an excursion to San Felipe are described in *Itinerary 2*.

–Before setting out, make sure you have a passport or ID, Mexican automobile insurance and – if you are not a US citizen or are heading south of Ensenada – a tourist permit. Also remember to make a reservation at San Quintín's Old Mill Hotel, tel: (619) 428-2779, for the overnight stop. Shoppers should note that US Customs demands receipts for any daily purchases exceeding $400 per person.–

As you drive into **Tijuana**, or cross the footbridge, you can see our first destination – a building topped with a big, glass piñata. This is **Mexitlan** (10am–6pm daily, closed Monday), an intriguing $23 million theme park containing enormous relief maps of all of Mexico with 150 of its major landmarks reproduced to scale on 6-m (20-ft) square platforms. It was created by Mexico's most famous architect, Pedro Ramirez Vazquez. Next door on 2nd Street (Calle Benito Juarez) is **Mercado Artesianas**, an arts and crafts market. Walk two blocks west and down Avenida Madero to the campy

Wax Museum whose eclectic subjects range from Madonna, Fidel Castro and the Pope, to Hernán Cortés, assorted Mexican revolutionary heroes and a gray-haired lady known as Tía Juana ('Aunt Jane'), the legendary owner of the rowdy cantina around which the city was founded.

Mexitlan

Now proceed another block west to the main drag, **Avenida Revolución**. Its one-time tawdry flavor is now sanitized but it is still the liveliest street, lined as it is with popular bars, night clubs, craft stores and clothing and jewelry shops mixed among the sarapes and sandals. If you want to leave your car and proceed on foot the favored parking lot is the inexpensive one by Woolworth's, Avenida Revolución at 2nd Street. Taxis will take you from the border to anywhere downtown at a very low cost.

Five blocks south on Revolución at 7th Street (Calle Galiano) is the stylish old **Jai Alai Fronton**. Jai Alai, a fast-moving game using a ball and a curved wicker basket, is played in the evening every Tuesday to Thursday. The main street continues south, joining the Boulevard Agua Caliente and running past the city's old bullring, the Sports Arena, which is the venue for most of the big concerts and other events, the best hotels and the famous Agua Caliente Racetrack, among whose regular clientele were once such stars as Charlie Chaplin, Jean Harlow, Al Jolson, Laurel and Hardy and Clara Bow. Fortunes were won and lost here at dice, blackjack and roulette.

But we turn left on 10th Street (Calle Sarabia) to head towards the river, watching for the distinctive giant golfball housing the concert hall and the 26-m (85-ft) high **Omnitheater** in which is shown daily at 2pm on a gigantic screen the English-language version of a film about Mexico's

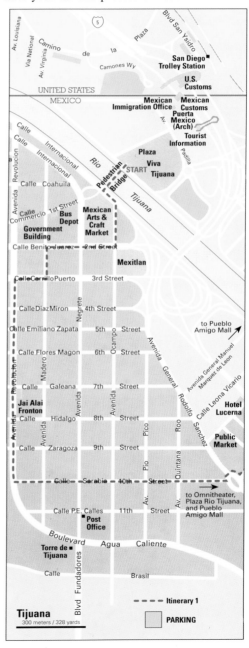

Warrior ready for battle

history and culture. Just before the river we cross Avenida Paseo de los Héroes. Statues of the heroes dot the *gloryetas* (traffic circles). Opposite the one of a man on horseback is our favored if unadventurous lunch place, the **Lucerna Hotel**, which is also a reliably comfortable place to stay. But first, back to Zona Rio.

Adjoining the Omnitheater is the ultra-modern **Tijuana Cultural Center** whose historical survey embraces Olmec stone heads; Aztec charts showing the god of the hour; a meticulous model of the 16th-century Aztec capital, Tenochtitlan; 19th-century boxes; a dramatic portrait of the fiery priest Father Miguel Hidalgo, saved from shooting by soldiers; skilfully embroidered Indian costumes, knives, money and folkcraft. Here also by the river is the **Plaza Rio Tijuana** shopping mall (open till 9pm) with 100 stores. It is the largest shopping center in northwestern Mexico where, Baja California being a free port, most goods cost less than in San Diego.

The distinctive red Tijuana Trolley runs continuously between the city's main sightseeing attractions from 10am–5pm every day, so take it if your feet are tired, but it's a pleasant stroll back northwards along Via Poniente and then across the river to Via Oriente. It will bring you to an older, funkier shopping center, **Pueblo Amigo**, which comes alive at night when crowds arrive to dine at the yellow and green **Señor Frog's** and numerous other restaurants. There is also a disco, a theater/concert hall and an ingenious mural which offers different pictures of a racing jockey when seen from around the room at various angles.

Riding the waves

Heading south, the *Cuota* (toll road) to Ensenada includes some fine ocean scenery. The *Libre* (free road) parallels the *Cuota* much of the way to Ensenada. About 27km (17 miles) south of the border, **Rosarito** is a somewhat commercialized beach town which first gained celebrity in 1927 when the newly-opened **Rosarito Beach Hotel** began to attract the movie crowd as well as other celebrities and even heads of state. The hotel features splendid indoor murals by Matias Santoyo and a large swimming pool and bar area above the gray, sandy beach. A green and white local bus operates on the old road to Tijuana every hour. Rosarito's recent acquisition is a pedicab which goes along the main street: originating in China it was brought to San Diego by a marine colonel who donated it to the town as an amusing tourist attraction.

Calafia

Calafia, an enormous complex of suites, bungalows, terrace bars and a reproduction of the old *Santa Maria* galleon, is sprawled over a headland 9km (5½ miles) south of Rosarito on the free road. Named after the legendary Amazonian queen, the resort is popular with young people, offering lots of noisy dancing at its outdoor disco. At the top of the so-called Fort of El Descanso is an attractive restaurant and bar. Rooms are inexpensive, and sometimes lucky visitors can spot passing whales, dolphins, sea lions and, more often, pelicans.

Nearby is **Las Rocas** with an attractive swimming pool, outdoor piano bar, jacuzzis and tennis courts, all in attractive gardens overlooking the sea. It's a good place to stop for lunch or a drink. And if you enjoy lobster, you'll be in your element in the so-called 'Lobster Village,' **Puerto Nuevo**, 10km (6 miles) to the south, where the New Port Baja Hotel, with its pool, jacuzzi, tennis courts, etc promises an ocean view from each of its 150 rooms.

On the *Libre* road overlooking the sea 65km (40 miles) south of the border, watch for the Plaza del Mar, with its distinctive painted Mayan pyramid above a garden containing reproductions of archaeological figures; La Misión, a big modern hotel with a well-stocked grocery store, and the charming La Fonda (a hotel with no telephone), whose restaurant and bar on a terrace patio are shaded by banana trees, large plants and foliage.

At La Fonda the free road turns inland towards the tiny village of **La Misión** where there are the fenced-off, crumbling ruins of the **San Miguel mission**. The ruins are only about 50m from the road but they are not immediately visible and are not signposted, so can easily be missed. The first boundary between the Dominican and Franciscan administrations was here at this mission but was later moved five leagues to the north when Father Palou carried a hardwood cross to the new boundary. The cross now stands on a high pedestal just below the enclosed grounds of La Misión school.

At **El Sauzal**, a community dominated by a fish cannery, Highway 3 runs 106km (66 miles) northeast to Tecate on the border (*see Itinerary 2*, pages 27–31) but we are stopping at Ensenada. As you enter the city of **Ensenada** (population 230,000) almost 113km (70 miles) south of the border, turn right off Highway 1 and drive up Avenida Alemán into the Chapultepec Hills, a high-rent district which offers an interesting overview of the city as you head down towards the harbor. Keep going straight ahead when you reach the bottom of the hill crossing Avenida Ruiz and then, beside the bus depot, Avenida Gastelum. This, the cheapest and funkiest

Today's catch for sale

area of town in which to shop and look around, is where almost every other store or bar seems to bear the name **Hussong** ('the bar that built a city'). The original venerable cantina, with its sawdust floor and old pictures, is a drinking place long popular with tourists from all over the world who have been pinning samples of their currency to the walls for over a century.

Among the numerous other restaurants around here, one of the pleasantest is the upstairs terrace in – what else? – Hussong Plaza. Between Ruiz and Gastelum, the restaurants Las Briausas and Los Amigos share an open patio. These are both on **Avenida López Mateos,** which is Ensenada's main shopping street. Before heading down further into town, walk to the end of Gastelum where you will see the immigration office and a tourist office, with the fish market behind them (open only until noon), and the busy sport-fishing piers.

A busy port, Ensenada is a regular stop for cruise ships and the furthest south that the vast majority of tourists penetrate. It stages off-road races, bike rides and regattas. Popular with fishermen, it tags itself 'the yellowtail capital of the world' with surf fishing along the rocky shoreline as well as organized trips from the sport-fishing piers. Ask at the tourist office if there is a tour at the **Bodegas de Santo Tomás winery**, located five blocks away at Avenida Miramar and 6th Street.

The **State Tourism Office** is on Avenida López Mateos, and there is another tourist information office on Boulevard Lázaro Cárdenas,

Magnificent stretch of coast

which heads south following the curve of the Bahía de Todos Santos, turning left to rejoin Highway 1 at the end of town. Note the 3.7-m (12-ft) high busts of former presidents Juarez, Hidalgo and Carranza in the **Plaza Cívica** on your right, and further down on your left, the Spanish Colonial-style **Centro Cívico**, formerly an elegant resort and casino. Ten kilometers (6 miles) south of here is Highway 3 which runs southeast, joining Highway 5 to San Felipe (*see Itinerary 2, pages 27–31*).

At Maneadero is the turn off, Highway 23, along the 16-km (10-mile) Punta Banda peninsula to **La Bufadora**, a watery blowhole that's quite an interesting sight (*bufa* means 'to snort'). Celia's Restaurant (which promotes its half-gallon margaritas), just before the main street, has a minimart and is a possible parking place if you don't want to negotiate the narrow street to the rocky ravine where incoming waves are forced into a narrow cleft, spraying spectators, who usually find it amusing. Sellers of onyx elephants, straw hats, cactus-shaped bottles, serapes, sugared churros and coconuts all vie for your attention. Parking is not that expensive in various unpaved lots, but there's nowhere to turn on the narrow main street. High tide is the best time to visit, of course, when the waves can spout 18m (60ft) in the air. (Consult the *Baja Sun* for tides timetable.) You can also take a cruise on a Royal Pacifico yacht from Ensenada Bay and see La Bufadora from the sea.

Near **Santo Tomás**, only ruins remain of the 18th-century mission, two of whose padres were killed by their Indian flock, but its vineyards are still here, greatly expanded. Earlier this century, at the nearby ranch of wealthy Arnie Babcock (his father built San Diego's fab-

La Bufadora

ulous Hotel Del Coronado), the original Baja Buggy was commissioned – and delivered the week after Arnie died. He had hired two ingenious mechanics, the Hunt Brothers, to create for him an extraordinary vehicle with high clearance and wheels 1.5m (5ft) apart, to ride the wagon tracks of what were then Baja's only 'roads.' The resulting vehicle, which was sold to an Ensenada man by Arnie's widow, was said to have been capable of driving – even racing – across ploughed fields at 100kph (60mph).

South of Colonet at **San Telmo de Abajo**, a graded dirt road, passable enough (in the dry season) heads eastwards to the sprawling **Meling Ranch**, which also has its own 1,220-m (4,000-ft) airstrip. Here you can stay in comfortable quarters, swim in the pool and ride horses into the **San Pedro Mártir Mountains**, a national park where deer live in the oak and pine forests. An observatory which

A forbidding fence

sits near the top of the mountains' highest peak, **Picacho del Diablo** (3,100m/10,154ft) was sited here because Baja – along with the west coasts of Africa and Chile – is one of the most cloud-free areas in the world.

'The sky is beautifully clear; the stars shine with the brilliancy of diamonds; the air is fragrant with the delicate odor of wildflowers; the stillness of death reigns over the camp in these profound solitudes... the very rocks and sands seem clothed with a garniture of celestial light,' enthused John Ross Browne in 1868, and apart from the construction of **the observatory**, very little has changed since then.

The farming region around **San Vicente** is rich in the oil-bearing jojoba plant and still a source of the delicious wild honey that was once a major Mexican export.

Virtually inaccessible are the minimal remains of the old San Pedro Mártir de Verona mission, but west of Highway 1, south of Camalu, are the crumbling adobe walls of the **Santo Domingo mission**, named for the founder of the Dominican order in 1775. The Santo Domingo river which rises high in the mountains above here is said to be the only one in all of Baja with a consistent flow throughout its entire length all year round.

Carry on from here to San Quintín, our overnight stop, which is 190km (118 miles) south of Ensenada.

An alternative route to the border towns of Tecate and Mexicali, and south to San Felipe.

–Highway 2 from Tijuana to Tecate 87km (54 miles) takes about one hour to drive. To get on to the libre (free) road, turn onto Boulevard Insurgentes at Boulevard Universidad. Mexicali is 144km (89 miles) east of Tecate. From Mexicali to San Felipe is 142 km (88 miles).–

You could also start this excursion from Ensenada, on Highway 3, beginning just to the north at El Sauzal and running 106km (66 miles) to Tecate, passing through vineyards on the boulder-strewn hills bordering the Guadalupe Valley, the center of Mexico's fast-growing wine business. Near the village of **Guadalupe** are a few remains of the last of the Baja missions to be built, which was prosperous for a short time because the valley had plenty of water. The mission had a garrison of soldiers which in 1836 repulsed an attack by Yuma Indians but Padre Caballero was forced out four years later. At the town of **Francisco Zara** the cemetery and museum are both devoted to the history of the Russian immigrants who colonized the vicinity at the turn of the century. The Guadalupe area claims to be the 'new Napa Valley' with a climate suitable for many different types of grapes, and its wine is worth sampling.

Tecate, the origin of whose name is disputed, is becoming popular with artists and writers but it's better known to visitors for its bakeries and the famous **Tecate Brewery**. Try a cheese and jalepeño *empanada* from the pink building called Mejor Pan, two blocks on the left past the Parque Hidalgo, the pleasant, tree-shaded main square. Three blocks west, the brewery, at Avenida Hidalgo and Calle Carranza, offers free tours from 9am–noon on Saturdays (tel: 665-4-1709).

Tecate to Mexicali: The initial section of this 143-km (89-mile) journey along

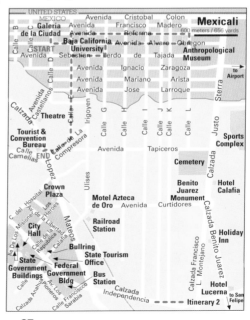

Highway 2 to Mexicali

Highway 2 is uncharacteristically green but is followed by the dry bed of Laguna Maccahui on which mysterious, ancient drawings have been found. The **Rumorosa** section of the highway with its sudden switchbacks, dramatic rock formations and steep descents is among the most spectacular drives in Baja and is quite awe-inspiring.

Like most state capitals, **Mexicali** is not very interesting from a tourist point of view and because the numerous one-way streets are not signposted or marked as such it is not easy to find your way around if you are driving. However, it's a sprawling, prosperous city, with shady, tree-lined streets and public parks. One of the things to see is the (free) **Galería de la Ciudad** (Monday to Friday 9am–8pm), in a lovely mansion that was once the governor's residence, at Avenida Alvaro Obregón and Calle D. Attractive homes can be seen around the university here and on the parallel Avenida

Reforma, where the **Museo Regional**, an anthropological museum, at the junction with Calle L, quite often seems to be closed. The **tourist office**, on Calzada López Mateos at Calle Camelias, may be able to give advice about opening hours and about other places of interest. In summer and fall rodeos (*charreadas*) are staged about 5km (3 miles) outside town on the road leading to the airport. The best motels are on **Justo Sierra Boulevard**, near the border in the northeastern part of town. These include the Motel La Siesta, and the more expensive Hotel Calafia, which has a pool. Many of the region's foreign-owned industrial plants are also in this area, close to the airport.

Kings of the road

Originally settled in 1898, Mexicali didn't come into its own until four years later when completion of the Imperial Canal brought water from the Colorado River for irrigation. For many years, the US-based Colorado River Land Company owned most of the valley, employing large numbers of Chinese immigrants to pick cotton, and it's still a place where Chinese restaurants (over 50 of them) predominate. Gambling, prostitution and drugs were rampant until gambling was banned in 1935. The following year much of the land was sold to Mexican farmers, who formed agricultural communities called *ejidos,* and in 1945 an international water treaty guaranteed Mexico irrigation water from the Colorado River.

One hour to the east, on Highway 8, is **Los Algodones**, a small farming community which was at its busiest when the Morelos Dam was built across the Colorado River in 1952. It is now the least used border crossing, but it's a pleasant enough little town, with most of the essential facilities. The dam, however, enabled almost half-a-million acres to be cultivated in the Mexicali Valley – mostly planted with olives and cotton (*algodon* means cotton).

After this small detour, which you may wish to omit, return to Mexicali and take Highway 5, which runs south to **San Felipe**. This is a smooth, wide road across desert for about three quarters of its 198-km (124-mile) run, with interesting vistas of low, friendly mountains. An elevated highway crosses Laguna Salada which has been mostly dry since the 1930s, but occasionally fills up when one of the delta tributaries overflows, unleashing a torrent and sometimes bringing fish in its wake. An unpaved but passable road running down the west side of Laguna Salada leads, after 65km (40 miles), to the lovely **Cañón de Guadalupe,** with its pools, waterfalls and hot springs around which a handful of camping sites have sprung up.

Vegetation in the desert

Emerging from a sandy no-mans-land about 200km (120 miles) south of the border, Highway 5 skirts the sea past a succession of trailer camp communities before entering the bay of San Felipe. The town's bus station is five long blocks from the waterfront. Across the desert to the west can be seen some of Baja's highest mountains, the Sierra de Juárez, and to the northeast on the Sonora coast of the 'Vermilion Sea' is the tiny fishing village of **El Golfo de Santa Clara** near where the Colorado River empties into the gulf. (Vermilion is the color of the microscopic marine life that sometimes tints the water.) Tidal waves as high as 9m (30ft) are not unknown here in this northern part of the gulf.

From a collection of shacks sheltered by a steep headland, San Felipe has grown to become a popular resort, although sport fishing

San Felipe

– for bass, sierra, corvina – is still the main attraction. Stroll along the waterfront and sample some seafood at one of the numerous counters. On the main street behind the *malecón* (waterfront), Cachanillas, its window filled with fish mobiles, is a nice place to eat. Just across the street is the boisterous Rockodile, a big, noisy bar with pool tables and an 'official' store selling eponymous T-shirts, mugs, etc. It stages parties and cheap drink nights with such specialties as 'everybody in shorts.' The slab-like El Cortez Motel which dominates much of the town's beach is more comfortable than it looks, and on the hill behind town is the slightly cheaper Travelodge which has a pool. About a mile south of town is the relatively expensive Hotel Las Misiones, a beach resort and tennis complex, in landscaped grounds. There are buses from here to Tijuana, Mexicali and Ensenada, but they are not very frequent, so it's advisable to check the times at the hotel.

Natural hot springs can be found in the desert west of San Felipe, notably at **Agua Caliente** (which means hot water), but a more adventurous trip is to take the recently paved 84-km (52-mile) road from San Felipe to Puertecitos. This leaves the sea shortly after the airport turnoff, traversing a monotonously barren plain with numerous dips (*vados*) in the highway, followed by scores of bone-jarring potholes. There is no gas station along the entire route. Dirt tracks leading to a succession of oceanside trailer camps are distinctively marked, each with its archway, twin cacti, or row of white-washed boulders; most have rental or for sale signs, and satellite dishes and solar panels abound. Eventually we see the blue bay ahead, sentinel rocks flanking one end. **Puertecitos** is delight-

Strolling into the sunset

fully higgledy piggledy, with no planning whatsoever. Trailers, makeshift sheds, and stone-built residences straggle cheek by jowl betwixt unpaved roads around the hillside. Some houses are adorned with stolen California street signs.

The Pemex station (which has no unleaded gas) appears deserted but somebody usually materializes when you blow your horn. The library and post office each occupy booths about 2.5m (8ft) high by 1.5m (5ft) wide. There is only one cafe, which doubles as a bar. There's a beach with palapas (straw umbrellas) for shade and makeshift cabins for rent, but townspeople bathe in shallow sea off the boat ramp at the far end of town. The sea is like warm bath water. At the entrance to Puertecitos, whose fascination lies largely in what its future inevitably holds, is a small but amazingly well-stocked store with everything from automobile oil to diapers, from Milk of Magnesia to canned Spam, kitchen

The Rockodile bar

utensils and ice-cold beer. It's also air-cooled and the best place to drink your beer or soda. A bus service is expected soon.

The present dirt road is about to be paved another 90km (56 miles) south beyond **Bahía de San Luis Gonzaga,** next in line for big-time resort development, with its beautiful bay whose baby waves lap a long, undisturbed beach. Beside the air strip a filtration system has been installed in the place which, 250 years ago, Jesuit Padre Fernando Consang found uninhabitable for lack of fresh water. For a while, after 1767, it became a coastal supply port for the last Jesuit mission, remote Santa María in the sierras to the southwest. Beyond the bay the present dirt highway will eventually be paved to **Punta Final** and then west through Las Arrastas to join Highway 1 south of Cataviña.

At present the only reliable way for ordinary automobiles to continue southwards down the peninsula is to go back through San Felipe, turning westward along Highway 3 about 50km (30 miles) north of the town and traveling up to Ensenada to join Highway 1. About 77km (48 miles) along the east-west leg, just before Valle de Trinidad, is the 35-km (22-mile) dirt road leading to **Mike's Sky Ranch,** a mountain resort with a pool, horses for hire and camping facilities, in the superb scenery of the San Pedro Mártir mountains, which are snow-clad from October to May.

An alternative way to enjoy the solitude and grandeur of the mountains comes at the village of **Ojos Negros** about 50km (32 miles) south of Ensenada, where a 44-km (27-mile) smooth but unpaved road leads to the national park (Parque Nacional Constitución de 1857) containing the pine-fringed **Laguna Hanson**.

San Quintín's Old Mill Hotel

3. San Quintín to Guerrero Negro

—San Quintín to Guerrero Negro is 414km (257 miles). This is a long trip through barren countryside, and the road is a little monotonous. Pack a picnic and cool drinks in case you get hungry and thirsty when there is nowhere convenient to stop.—

Strung out along the highway, about two miles apart, the small towns of **San Quintín** and Lázaro Cárdenas at first seem to have little to offer except shops, restaurants and other commercial enterprises. But a right turn at Lázaro Cárdenas leads to the ocean and the magnificent, shallow bays which are a mecca for fishermen and clamdiggers but so far appreciated by few others. The Santo Domingo river empties into the sea just north of the bay where an oyster farm has been established. Another unpaved turnoff, south of **Lázaro Cárdenas,** leads to the main bay and your overnight stop, the **Old Mill Hotel,** where only the activities of early-rising fisherfolk disturb the tranquility. Hundreds of swaggering seagulls gather to watch the catch being eviscerated at sunset. Join them there, then have dinner in the excellent restaurant.

Both the Old Mill and the **Old Pier Hotel** further down the lagoon are reminders that once this area was colonized by an English land company which tried unsuccessfully to harvest crops and grind corn but went bankrupt for lack of rain. The names of these almost forgotten pioneers are recorded on a group of windswept graves by the shore. Camping on Bahía de San Quintín's wild peninsula, fishing and digging for 'chocolate-tipped' clams, is a favorite pastime of the cognoscenti.

Make an early start in the morning and head 58km (36 miles) south, where **El Rosario**, with its killer bend on the highway, breaks the monotony of more than 160km (100 miles) of sparsely populated desert. Ruins of the old mis-

Crafts for sale

A miners' graveyard

sion, abandoned in 1832, lie just over 3km (2 miles) southwest of the little town, which boasts little more than a Pemex station, a motel and a few cafés. The terrain is littered with the rusted hulks of crashed cars – too expensive to be towed hundreds of miles for repairs, they are usually left to be cannibalized by other motorists – and by thousands of those spidery cirio trees unique to Baja. The cirio trees, actually *idria columnaris*, bear tiny yellow flowers in season, but for much of the year they are devoid of decoration. They are sometimes referred to as boojum trees, after the mythical species described by Lewis Carroll in *The Hunting of the Snark.*

The terrain conforms to the popular image of Baja, a land preserving 'scraps of men's dreams: ruined missions, adobe walls blasted by the abrasive wind, trails that lead nowhere, bleached bones, abandoned mines, wrecked machinery,' as the writer William Weber Johnson once colorfully portrayed it.

At San Augustín is the turnoff, east 16km (10 miles) to **El Marmol**, site of a now-abandoned onyx-mining operation discovered in the 1890s. The Smithsonian Institute's George Merrill described seeing huge blocks of material 'with ever-varying shades of color... peculiarly delicate (and with) a wonderful uniformity in quality. Pearl-white, delicate rose tints and light greens are the most common, quite unique and wonderfully beautiful.' When the mine was operating the stone was cut by hand into blocks up to five tons in weight, taken by truck 80km (50 miles) west to Santa Catarina, then shipped to San Diego for cutting and polishing.

Silent screen star Theda Bara is said to have ordered a block of onyx from El Marmol, which she had made into a bathtub with gold faucets. Onyx is a very hard stone which polishes easily, is resistant to stain and is often banded with green, brown or occasionally rose-red. It is formed, like limestone and marble, from subterranean springs which bubble to the surface, depositing a lime crust.

Back on the highway, sudden flocks of little birds dart perilously across the road in front of your car and deeply rutted sandy tracks mined with sharp rocks lead off the road and into the wilderness. Three kilometers (2 miles) west on one of these trails are the ruins of **San Fernando**, the mission founded by Father Junípero Serra before he began his work north of San Diego.

Gigantic boulders, many of them irresistible to graffiti pests, carpet the land, and at **Cataviña** – an unexpected oasis with a Pemex station – they have been employed as the rear wall of several makeshift homes. The last of the Jesuit missions, **Santa María**, where Serra met with Captain Gaspar de Portola in May 1769 to begin their expedition to the north, is 23km (14 miles) east over a rocky trail. Although abandoned almost 200 years ago its adobe

Revenge of the fish

walls are well preserved and it is scheduled for restoration. The Hotel La Pinta in Cataviña is a good place to stop for lunch.

South of Cataviña the boulder-strewn countryside continues. Heading southeast the road climbs over the 820m (2,690ft) summit of Sierra Columbia, then drops into the arid lake bed of **Laguna Chapala**. Tall cirio abound as do the cardon cactus (clusters of grooved, thorny, leafless perpendicular branches that can grow to 12m/40ft) and the pink-blossomed elephant tree whose stubby trunk retains its moisture for years. Ahead are the windswept wastes of the **Vizcaíno Desert** where, surprisingly, as many as eighty species of plants turn out to be edible, despite the fact that the region is lucky to get 25cm (10 inches) of rain a year – in the years that it rains at all.

Cactus was always a source of nourishment for the Indians who would spoon out the pulp, and dry it in the sun. Apart from relishing the juicy pitahaya fruit, they would also devour seeds from mesquite and paloverde, as well as salt grass and eelgrass. The cardon or giant cactus has inedible fruit, but it produces black seeds which can be dried and toasted. Missionaries discovered that the juice, when boiled and condensed, could produce a healing balsam. They also found that the sweet potato-like hearts of the agaves could be roasted to make them safe for eating.

It is only 20 years since Highway 1, running all the way from northern to southern Baja, was completed and at **San Ignacito** the two work crews met. A small marker commemorates the spot where the meeting took place.

At **El Crucero**, an unpaved road leading northeast to the Gulf Coast passes the short-lived Misión Calamuje, of which virtually nothing remains. Sixteen kilometers (10 miles) further south is the turnoff to Bahía de los Angeles (*see Itinerary 4, pages 37–9*).

Home away from home

A 42-m (135-ft) high steel marker, **Monumento Aguila,** marks the boundary between northern and southern Baja and, 183m (200 yards) beyond, there is an inspection station for fruit and vegetables. Here is where, if you are without a car and speak a little Spanish, you might hitch a ride with a trucker. About 40 trucks, mostly owned by big companies, ply the Trans-Peninsular Highway constantly, making the 2,400km (1,500-mile) round trip to the border and back in three or four days. Some of these long-distance drivers have been making the trip for 20 years, and all of them know each other, talk constantly over CB radios and exchange flickers of lights and hand signals as they pass.

Guerrero Negro, our destination, gets its name from a British whaling ship, the *Black Warrior,* wrecked off the coast here in 1858 and never recovered. The bus stops on the highway a mile east of town. As you walk along Boulevard Zapata you will first pass the Malarrimo Trailer Park, next to the Malarrimo Motel and restaurant, a pretty place which does good Mexican dishes and seafood, and runs some of the best whale-watching tours in the area. You then come to two budget motels, the El Morro and the Las Dunas. If you are traveling by bus, try to check the schedules to avoid being stranded here unexpectedly.

Thousands of shallow saltwater ponds here, from which the sun evaporates the water, produce 5 million tons of salt per month for export, one-third of the world's supply. But the town is even better known for **Scammon's Lagoon**, at the end of a dirt road several miles south of town past the salt evaporating ponds. This is where for centuries whales have come from the chilly Bering Sea to breed in the warm, shallow bay. About 1,800 gray whales now gather off the Baja coast, about the same number as at their peak in 1850. From January to March each year they can be seen cavorting in the calm waters of the lagoon.

Altogether there are about 20,000 of these whales in the Pacific (none in the North Atlantic). They are about 10.5–

19th-century whaling fleet

14.5m (35–47ft) long, the females slightly bigger, and many live for 25 years. In the 1840s European and American whalers hunted these waters for the giant creatures who, although capable of swimming 8,000km (5,000 miles) to mate and calve, are helpless against human predators.

The most famous of the whalers was Captain Charles Scammon, born in Maine in 1825 and only 28 when he first took charge of a California whaling ship. Discovering one day the whales' secret

Whales in the lagoon

lagoon, he collected hundreds of barrels of oil by slaughtering all the mammals he could find. Inevitably he was followed and imitated by all the other whalers. Mother whales with the babies they had just delivered after almost a year's gestation were particularly helpless targets as they frolicked in the shallows or at the mouths of bays. Scammon, who seems to have had ice in his veins, kept extensive logs of the whales he killed and later published a work on marine mammals.

In his 1860 log book he noted: '...the objects of pursuit were found in large numbers and here the scene of slaughter was exceedingly picturesque and unusually exciting, especially on a calm morning, when the mirage would transform not only the boats and the crews into their fantastic imagery, but the whales as they sent forth their towering spouts of aqueous vapor, frequently tinted with blood, would appear greatly distorted.'

A decade later the captain was at it again, boasting in *Overland Monthly* how easy it had been to kill the 5-m (16-ft) long elephant seal (some of which weighed as much as three tons) which by that time – 1870 – had been all but exterminated for their oil.

One colony of these seals has survived on remote **Guadalupe Island,** which it shares with a few fishermen and an increasing numbers of admiring tourists. The Mexican government has declared the island a protected area, an enlightened policy that may eventually restore it to something like the pristine shape it was in before the whalers arrived with their omnivorous goats and cats. It was once 'a naturalist's dream,' one writer declared, with its rich, unique, flora and fauna and dense groves of cypress, pine and palm.

It was at Guerrero Negro, in 1972, that Mexico established the world's first whale sanctuaries to which today's hunters come armed only with cameras. An unpaved road leading off Highway 1 about 10km (6 miles) south of town leads to a whale-watching site at the edge of the lagoon but, of course, there are also organized, but rather expensive, tours that get closer by boat. Taxi drivers, who wait where

Whale-watch guide

Watching whales at play

the bus stops on the highway, can usually steer you to these tours. To get to the lagoon, follow signs to Parque Natural de la Ballena Gris/Gray Whale National Park. When you reach the observation point a small fee may or may not be requested. There is an observation tower on the shore; bring binoculars as the whales may be some way off. Binoculars will also be useful for spotting a variety of birdlife en route – cormorants, herons and pelicans.

'There is something about our notions of recreation that always merits examination,' wrote author Doug Peacock, on the curious custom of observers trekking to quite remote places to intrude 'on a species who didn't ask to be so closely watched while they make love and give birth.'

4. Bahía de los Angeles

–This is a fisherman's paradise and a true beauty spot, but there is not much to do except fish and admire the view. Be warned that the roads are bad, but see it before modernization and development changes its character.–

Eighteen kilometers (10 miles) beyond El Crucero on Highway 1, 105km (65 miles) south of Cataviña, is the turnoff road to Bahía de los Angeles. Although paved for all of its 68km (42 miles) it is dangerously potholed, although somewhat better than the undeveloped track leading off it southwards to the well-preserved mission of **San Francisco de la Borja**, founded by the wealthy Spanish

Bahía de los Angeles

Borja (or Borgia) family in the 1750s. That is a trip which should only be attempted in a four-wheel-drive vehicle. We will carry on to **Bahía de los Angeles**, which sounds idyllic, but is actually little more than a dusty backwater, a flat, scorchingly hot village with rutted, unpaved streets. The mountains to the west, and the azure waters of the bay provide a beautiful setting, but the area is really a mecca for those launching a boat or joining a fishing expedition. Bahía de los Angeles is another place destined for major development over the next few years, which will improve its facilities and its access, but will inevitably change its atmosphere. It has a miniscule museum and a handful of cafes and hotels, of which the best is **Villa Vita** with its small pool and a restaurant/bar. Opposite, overlooking the boat ramp, is an interesting building which looks like a revolving restaurant on stilts but doesn't move

and is actually a private residence. In the early months of the year grunion – the smelt-like fish that, around the full moon, come ashore in early evening to spawn – can be observed on the seashore north of town.

Dolphins can often be seen in the bay and the waters teem with fish (yellowtail, grouper, cabrilla) and thus Bahía is near-heaven to those sporting souls who can use their boats to visit two of the largest islands in the gulf, the uninhabited 56-km (35-mile) long **Isla Angel de la Guardia** offshore and 1210-sq km(467-sq mile) **Tiburón**, where seals nest along the northeastern coast and the interior mountain peaks top 1220m (4,000ft). Between them is tiny **Isla Raza**, a rare bird sanctuary visited only with special permission.

Tiburón's plentiful water supplies support sheep and deer in an interior valley as well as hundreds of plant species. These include the viznaga, a barrel cactus almost 4m (12ft) high, whose thorns can be used as knitting needles, tooth brushes, or toothpicks, as well as the opuntia or nopal plant whose pulp, inner rind and tender leaves are often baked or stewed. Transplanted from Europe by the missionaries, it grew well in Baja's arid soil.

'It is truly remarkable,' writes Clavigera, 'that (these) plants have more juice in the arid places than other kinds of trees have in damp places. But I am persuaded that these plants are juicier because they transpire less and they transpire less because they do not have leaves. Therefore it must be conjectured that the Creator denied leaves to these plants because he destined them to live in dry countries.'

The Indians did have one favorite food and during the late summer season it was their most valuable food source. This is a red, peach-sized fruit, the pitahaya, ripe for picking from the spiky cereus cactus between June and September, if it doesn't rain too much. It blossoms, ironically, only in the most arid places. There are two types of pitahaya fruit, one sweet and one bitter. The trunk grows scarcely a foot from the ground with a series of parallel, arm-thick branches growing up to 3m (10ft) or more in height and producing woody tubes that can be burned as torches when dry. Lovely, odorless white flowers are succeeded by a sweet fruit with small seeds, whose rind is covered with closely-set, strong thorns. Eating it stains the urine red. In southern

A prickly perch

Baja, the fruit, pulled from the plant with a hooked stick into a net (and the thorns carefully removed), is gathered from June through August, and slightly later in the north.

The season is followed in September, October and sometimes even November by the fruit of the tajua, a similar species found on the branches of a spreading cactus near the beach. It bears white and red flowers and orange-sized fruit with a pleasant bitter-sweet flavor. Another plant, the ghakil or gambullo, yields a similar but smaller, and less tasty fruit. Part of the Indians' early diet was piñon nuts, collected from trees found only in Baja and parts of California, and ground into meal. The hearts of an edible mescal plant were also roasted and eaten.

Father Clavigera's history is notable for its meticulous descriptions of the flora and fauna of this barren land, and his keen observations remain largely valid two centuries later. The most widely distributed fruit in the southern part of Baja, he writes, is the ciruela, similar to a plum, which blossoms in April or May, with fruit maturing in August to September. The kernel tastes like the nut of a pistachio but the fruit is harsh to the taste 'good only to the palate of those wretched Indians who are accustomed to eat whatever offers itself to them.' About the Indians, Clavigera

Miner's cart

observed: 'In regard to their souls... they are not different from the rest of the sons of Adam. Those who have been brought up in the wilds have those vices and imperfections which are consistent with savage life in all countries.'

South of Bahía de los Angeles an unpaved road, in parts as rutted as a washboard, heads some 60km (38 miles) through the mountains and back to the sea at **Playa San Rafael**, passing through **Los Flores,** an abandoned silver mine which is said to have produced $2 million-worth of silver. When the naturalist author Joseph Wood Krutch visited in the 1940s he found that the only building of which four walls still stood was the jail which drunken miners passed on their way home and in which they would be confined by the jailer to sleep it off until morning. The hard-to-reach **Bahía de San Rafael** is becoming very popular with fishermen in the know, who report record catches, in addition to the clams just waiting to be picked up. The tidal waters between the coast and the trio of Salsipuedes Islands are dangerous. An alternative route to San Rafael is from the west, taking a turning off Highway 1 through **El Arco**, but this route requires a four-wheel-drive vehicle.

From Bahía de los Angeles you must drive back northwest to rejoin Highway 1 just north of **Punta Prieta** from which it is 130km (80 miles) to the massive steel structure which marks the boundary between the states of Baja California Norte and Baja Sur.

–Call Oscar Fischer at La Posada Motel (tel: 685-4-00-13) in San Ignacio if you want to discuss making a trip to see the Indian cave paintings. It is 142km (88 miles) to San Ignacio, a further 73km (45 miles) to Santa Rosalia. Make sure you have plenty of food and water, and spare gasoline for emergencies is a good precaution. Petrol stations, stores and restaurants are few and far between. Be prepared to encounter some poor roads once you leave the main highway.–

This route takes us from Baja Norte to Baja Sur. Don't forget to reset your clocks if you come in winter, because the time zones change and the south is an hour ahead. In the summer it remains the same. The area south of Guerrero Negro is probably the most barren section of the peninsula, a plateau about 40km (25 miles) wide and 480km (300 miles) long, lying near the Pacific coast. It is volcano country, as can be seen by the reddish-brown cinder cone rocks, and sulphur has been found between the scattered cattle ranches in the low cactus-covered hills. The volcano, **Las Tres Virgenes**, north of Santa Rosalia, has been active in this century. An enemy to missionaries and Indians alike in this mountainous region was a toxic shrub known as *yerba de la flecha* (the arrow plant), which has multiple branches and long green leaves resembling those of the willow. Merely resting in its shade can cause intense burning of the eyes and body and in Sonora it was used by Indians

Santa Gertrudis mission

as a poison with which to tip their arrows.

Santa Gertrudis, one of the best preserved missions, is down a very bad road that branches off the highway 27½km (17 miles) south of Guerrero Negro, turning southeast at the former gold mining town of **El Arco**. It dates from 1751, half a century after the first mission was established at Loreto. Jorge Retz, a German Jesuit who had spent a year at San Ignacio learning the Cochimi language, opened the mission, aided by a blind Indian architect named Andres Comanaji, whose skill, reported the Jesuit historian Francisco Xavier Clavigera, 'was such that his touch was substituted for his lack of sight.' When the buildings were completed, Father Retz cut a canal from a spring 2km (1¼ miles)

The bells of Santa Gertrudis

Road to Santa Gertrudis

away, and planted trees and grape vines. The wine he made was stored in stone containers, because there were no casks available.

Under the Franciscans the mission claimed 1,000 residents, half of them children. While being spiritually nourished they were also being weaned off their normal cuisine and encouraged to eat meat, for the mission raised hundreds of cattle, sheep and goats. For centuries the Indians had lived on what they could find including (according to Clavigera) 'bitter roots, scrawny and tasteless dates, insipid fruits, locusts, lizards, snakes, green caterpillars, worms of all kinds, spiders and other insects.' Gradually the diet of the native people improved as the missionaries planted more crops: wheat, rice, melons, pumpkins, beans, oranges, lemons, limes, figs, pomegranates and grapes, as well as cotton to make cloth. In 1722 and 1723, however, thousands starved to death when immense plagues of locusts devastated most of the crops.

To the northeast is the gulf at **San Francisquito** which is renowned among fishermen for the rich shoals of yellowtail which appear offshore in winter. To reach it you must take Highway 18 to El Arco, then continue northeastwards for some 80km (50 miles). The beautiful white-sand beaches are dotted with colorful shells and although the oyster beds are long gone (piles of empty shells among the dunes testify to their one-time abundance) the shoreline is rich in clams and other shellfish.

But you may choose to go west instead: from Vizcaíno Junction, 75km (47 miles) south of Guerrero Negro on Highway 1, a passable road heads back northwest up the **Vizcaíno Peninsula**, a six-hour drive, to **Bahía Tortuga**, well known to sports-fishermen by its anglicized name of **Turtle Bay**. There is a simple motel, the Vera Cruz. Remote communities such as Bahía Asunción, Puerto Nuevo, tiny San Benito and most of the small islands subsist on fishing, particularly for lobster and abalone.

A lift to the caves

The larger island, **Isla Cedros,** where pirate ships used to lie in wait for the Manila galleons, now ships salt which arrives by barge from Guerrero Negro. This is a popular base for visiting sports-fishermen from the San Diego area.

If you are continuing south down Highway 1, you will reach a turning to **Santa Marta** and **San Francisco de la Sierra**, about 45km (28 miles) north of San Ignacio. There are some Indian cave paintings – giant figures high on the cave walls in brown, red and black – painted in colors apparently made from mineral earth found near the Tres Virgenes volcano. Local people act as guides to the cave in an area now declared an official Archaeological Zone and you can take mule trips from the village to the caves (ask at La Posada Motel in San Ignacio) but rattlesnakes and scorpions occasionally make the trip a little intimidating, and it is also quite expensive.

Mystery writer Erle Stanley Gardner, who wrote half a dozen books about Baja, which he also explored from the air by plane, helicopter and Goodyear blimp, wrote that when he visited the caves locals told him he had been the first visitor the village had seen. A UCLA anthropologist who accompanied him, Dr Clement Meigham, said they inspected nine caves of which the biggest – 152m (500ft) long – contained 130 portrayals of men, deer, rabbits and bighorn sheep. He estimated they had been painted around AD1100.

Gardener also wrote about certain 'lost mines' whose legends dated back to the days when the Indians, noting how important gold was to the Spaniards, had stored their hoards in caves which they sealed off with an avalanche of boulders.

San Francisco de la Sierra

Legends of hidden treasure may be apocryphal but are understandable in such mysterious isolated terrain. Rumors dating back to the expulsion of the Jesuits in 1767 were based on a supposedly secret order from their superiors in Madrid to 'Submit peacefully but leave no trace of your wealth.' Ever since, people have searched for spots where such treasures might be stored – in a 'lost Mission Santa Isabel' – but given the poverty-stricken conditions under which the fathers worked in this barren land, it is unlikely that such a mission, or treasure, actually exists.

If you are traveling by bus, it will stop on the highway a couple of miles from **San Ignacio**, where taxis are waiting. As you enter the town notice where an underground river emerges as a small lake. People rave about the town's beauty but in truth it's a tiny town, a tropical oasis almost hidden amid thousands of date-bearing palm trees, plus some vineyards and orange trees. Its small square, lined with shady laurel trees, is dominated by the impressive **San Ignacio Mission**, erected in 1786 by Dominican Padre Juan Christomo Gomez, who was distinguished for sav-

San Ignacio Mission

ing all but three or four of his congregation by injecting them with a live vaccine during a smallpox epidemic. The lava rock mission with its 1.2-m (4-ft) thick walls and arched ceiling replaced an earlier Jesuit mission dating from 1728. Two mini-markets, one also selling clothing, are on the square, but there is not much else. A solitary restaurant, La Tota, is just off one end and there are a couple of taco stands.

A decrepit but inexpensive place to stay, Oscar Fischer's La Posada Motel, half a mile southeast of the plaza on Calle Carranza, is where you can arrange the expensive but fascinating excursion trips to see the Indian cave paintings. Or try the La Pinta Hotel, on the way into the plaza. It costs more than La Posada but has air conditioning and a pool. There is an air strip near San Ignacio, one of a number listed in a book by two intrepid pilots, Allen and Phyllis Ellis, who visited and documented most of these remote sites in the 1960s when aviation gasoline cost 64¢ a gallon, and the authors wrote that they could live on a couple of dollars a day. Not all the air strips were hazard-free and few were maintained. 'Debris-laden beach requires alertness on landing' was a typical piece of advice from the authors.

The original San Ignacio mission was the creation of the Jesuit priest Juan Bautista Loyando who had studied the Cochimi language in Loreto before founding the Mission of San Ignacio Kadakaaman almost in the middle of the peninsula in 1728. A wealthy descendant of one of the Jesuit founders, Father Loyando dedicated 10,000 pesos of his own money to establishing San Ignacio. The land was fertile, with plenty of water, enabling the mission to plant date palms, fruit trees and grape vines, and even raise herds of cattle and sheep. The padres immediately called the bluff of the *guamas* (medicine men) who provided much of the opposition to the early missionaries. Dressed in long garments of human hair with painted faces and wearing headdresses of sparrowhawk feathers, the *guamas* sometimes wore crowns of deer tails and had two strings of deer hoofs hanging from their waists.

'In curing the sick the *guamas*' chief instrument was a piece of wood with marks on it from which he made a show of reading the nature of the illness,' Dunne writes in *Black Robes in Lower California*, recounting how the medicine man would put a thorn or thistle in his mouth and pretend to draw it from the patient through a smoke-filled tube placed on the afflicted part.The payment for the 'cure' would be bundles of human hair but people were also obliged to donate feathers, the first and best fruits of the season, the finest fish and the biggest seeds.

From San Ignacio, Highway 1 offers many dramatic switchback curves until the coast is reached 73km (45 miles) later at **Santa Rosalia,** a former company town, founded and badly exploited by the French in the 1880s to mine copper. When supplies ran out in 1954 the El Boleo company abandoned the town, which now produces manganese. The small, wooden houses from the French era give it a curiously anomalous look; author John Steinbeck called it the 'least Mexican-style city' he had seen. A prefabricated iron church built by Gustav Eiffel – the designer of the world-renowned Parisian tower and the framework for the Statue of Liberty – won second prize at the 1889 Universal Exposition in Paris and was then taken apart and packed in crates, for shipment to Africa. After being rejected by the African company for which the ant-proof structure had been built, it was bought by the El Boleo company and taken to Santa Rosalia, where an exterior plaster wall was added. Situated behind the plaza, it has small painted glass windows.

As you come into town from the highway the **Sematur** dock, from which ferries

Rugged resident

El Boleo bakery

run to and from Guaymas three times each week, is on the right-hand side, opposite some abandoned caves cut horizontally into a cliff that borders the road.

Two main streets lead gently uphill from the main square, **Constitución** and **Alvaro Obregón**, with other parallel streets at left and right. Most of the activity and eating places are on Obregón. These include the tiny Restaurant Tokio (Mexican food), Cha Cha (hamburger counter), and Don Dragon (which opens at 5pm), a two-story steak house at Constitución and Calle 7. Also on Obregón at Calle 4 is the El Boleo bakery ('World famous bread,' a sign claims) which also sells tasty jelly doughnuts.

Using a handmade squid lure known as a *potera* – a weighted piece of plastic atop rings of thin, sharp metal spikes – fishermen used to bring in tons of squid every week from off the coast but the supply has unaccountably dried up over the past few years. Heading down the coastal highway you can see **Isla San Marcos**, a major source of gypsum which is mined by a joint US-Mexican combine. It has a population of about 700.

Forty-eight kilometers (30 miles) northwest of Mulegé at **San Borjitas** are more caves, with paintings of several dozen figures: men and women, fish, deer. The men, pierced with arrows, have arms outstretched. At present, these caves are not accessible to the public.

When the Santa Rosalia mission was finally established Father Juan Manuel Basaldua planned a rough road to Loreto, 80km (50 miles) away. But first he turned his attention to **Mulegé**, an oasis 61km (38 miles) south of Santa Rosalia where Juan de Ugarte, one of the most resourceful of the Jesuit fathers, had made unsuccessful attempts to establish a mission in 1704. The present mission dates from 1766.

Sign of good fishing

–Explore Mulegé, with its museum and mission and have lunch at the beach restaurant El Almeja, before setting off on the 136-km (84-mile) journey to Loreto.–

Where the bus stops at the entrance to **Mulegé**, as Calles Moctezuma and Rubio meet the main highway, the sign proclaims H MULEGÉ. The H stands for heroic, and is a reference to an October day in 1847, during the Mexican-American war, when two US ships entered the harbor but were frightened away by a locally orchestrated subterfuge. On October 2 each year the town, situated in a lush valley with tropical birds, date palms, mango trees and fresh water wells, celebrates the bravery and quick-thinking of Heroic Mulegé.

Stay at either the pretty Las Casitas or the slightly larger Hotel Hacienda, which are neighbors on Calle Madero a few yards from the town square. The former is nicer, the latter has a pool and both have restaurants. Mountain bike rentals and trips to the cave paintings can be booked at the Hacienda. Opposite the hotels is Mulegé Divers (Madero 45) where you can rent equipment for undersea exploration. On the square is a supermarket and the post office. The laundromat is at Zaragoza and Moctezuma streets, and you may be glad to find it if you have been traveling for a while without stopping.

Date palm grove

From the square walk up Moctezuma, turn right and climb 95 steps up the hill to the fortress-like **museum** — a jail until 1975 — whose artifacts include the desk of the late mystery writer Erle Stanley Gardner, an antique typewriter from the old mining office in Santa Rosalia, a bag made from bulls' testicles and pictures relating to that historic day in 1847 when the barely-armed citizens of Mulegé scared off the potential invaders by constructing dummies of armed men on a hill overlooking the bay.

The Sea of Cortez, into which the river empties, is about one mile down the unpaved road where, on the north side of the river, is Ramon's delightful beach restaurant **El Almeja** (The Clam). To reach the delightful Hotel Serenidad you must head down Zaragoza under the highway bridge and along the river's other (south) bank which is lined with houses and RV trailers sheltering under makeshift roofs, the vehicles serving as permanent homes, with the surrounding area as their open-air patios. There's an attractive view from the little **lighthouse**.

Owned by an American named Don Johnson, the **Hotel Serenidad** has comfortable cabanas, a large swimming pool, a bar and a restaurant which hosts Mulegé's major weekly event, a Saturday night

View of Mulegé

pig roast. The pigs have been fed on dates. For reservations and also to book for the fishing excursions that start from the beach beside the hotel, tel: 3-01-11. Adjoining is an airstrip sometimes used by the hotel's more affluent guests. Two pleasantly shaded RV camps, the Orchard and the Oasis, and an eating place, La Jungla Bambu, sit on the riverside below the hotel.

To visit the **mission** go down Zaragoza and turn right under the highway along the path through the mango and guava forest. It's well worth making the 20-minute walk. The mission, built in 1766, is on a hill with a rocky bluff nearby offering a lovely view with the muddy river winding through groves of palm trees.

It was in the hills near here, almost half a century before the mission was founded, that Father Juan de Ugarte, by then President of the Missions, discovered the hardwood trees called *guaribo*. He hired a master shipbuilder who helped him build 'the most beautiful, the sturdiest and the best constructed sailing vessel ever known in Lower California.' In the *Triunfo de la Cruz,* he then explored the gulf for more mission sites. The Baja missions eventually possessed 20 boats, used to transport supplies and bring in new missionaries. Everything sent from Mexico went via the port of Matanchel and thence to Loreto where a Jesuit procurator handled the distribution to the various missions.

In 1720 Father Ugarte, who had been described by his colleague Salvatierra as 'the Atlantic, the Pillar of California to whom after God is due the conversion of the Indians of these Missions,' founded the La Paz mission. At almost the same time another one, Guadalupe, was being built at Guasinapi in the mountains above Mulegé, in the region where the timber for the boat had been cut. The German padre Everado Helen was welcomed by the Indians, who came to the mission from miles

The mission outside Mulegé

Bahía Concepción

around, but before he would allow them to receive baptism the padre insisted that they gave up all the relics of their former superstitions and beliefs.

In 1722 a plague of locusts wiped out almost all the crops and some people survived only because of the mission's supply of corn. Many Indians died from eating locusts, for lack of anything else. This mission, only the foundations of which remain, is virtually inaccessible, some four hours' hike from San José de Magdalena.

South of Mulegé the highway skirts the shore, offering tantalizing glimpses of delightful coves and bays which are only accessible by a four-wheel-drive vehicle. Framed to the east by a northward-pointing peninsula, the 40-km (25-mile) long **Bahía Concepción** is famous for its enticing camping beaches, all with simple facilities such as toilets, trash cans and sheltering palapas. Most of the rocks between beaches are occupied by morose pelicans gazing silently at the sea. The pelican rookeries in the rocky coves of the gulf have fared better than those of their cousins on the Pacific Coast, where survival is apparently more hazardous, but many birds are regular commuters over the intervening mountains. Needless to say, fishermen at sea are avid followers of the hovering pelicans.

Pensive pelicans

Sixty-five kilometers (40 miles) across the mountains northwest of Loreto in the middle of the peninsula, are three small missions sharing the name **Comondú** and, northwest of these, **La Purísima**, built in 1717, which eventually, under Padre Nicolás Tamaral, became the most populous of the missions, with 2,000 residents.

The padre described his Indians as being tall and robust, with dark chestnut-colored hair extending well below the shoulders. The men went naked or nearly so, women wore skirts made from twigs or grasses, suspended by a thong from the waist. Some women wore skins of wild animals, which might be painted with figures in red, yellow or white. They used pottery dishes for cooking and storing food, the bladder of a deer for carrying water. They roasted seeds, acorns, jojobas or piñon nuts in tightly woven baskets. By adding sand to hot coals in the baskets they prevented them from burning. The men hunted for food, using bows and arrows, or spears tipped with chipped stone.

A secondary road north from Ciudad Constitución (see *Itinerary 7*, pages 51–6) to **Poza Grande**, and then off onto unpaved roads for about 65km (40 miles) is the easiest access to what remains of these missions but there is a rough road just south of Loreto and another, better, one some 75km (47 miles) south of Mulegé. The communities of Comondú and La Purísima are pleasant little spots, surrounded by palm groves, vineyards and citrus crops — a contrast to the barren landscape which surrounds them. They once produced considerable amounts of liquor, olive oil and leather products, but lost much of their prosperity after being bypassed by Highway 1.

For bus travelers, the **Loreto** bus station is at the top of town where the Paseo Pedro de Ugarte meets Highway 1 and there is a mini food market just across the street. If you have heavy luggage you will need to take a taxi for the half dozen blocks into town, unless you choose to stay at the **Motel Salvatierra**, which is only one block away.

On your way into town you will pass Calle Allende, where there's a post office and a big supermarket just before Hidalgo branches off. Next comes the mission and the town square, the **Plaza Cívica**, where the impressive town hall proclaims that Loreto was the first capital of the Californias. Just behind it is the tourist office and one block away, on Hidalgo, the Hotel Plaza.

Right beside **Misión Nuestra Señora de Loreto**, the oldest mission in the Americas, is a statue of Juan María Salvatierra who remained here for 20 years, tirelessly overseeing most of the other padres, converting souls, and never finding any task too small for his attention. In a letter to a Guadalajara colleague in 1699, he remarked: 'You will be so good as to forgive me if I do not write at greater length; a swelling on the hand caused by putting it in the mud to show my fellow Californians how to make adobe, makes it hard to write.'

The mission, which will be 300 years old in 1997 is a glorious sight today, having been restored after extensive hurricane damage. The towers were restored with the lottery winnings of a former padre. The adjoining **museum** (open a few hours most mornings

The oldest mission in the Americas

Hotel Misión

and afternoons) displays religious paintings, saddles, some elaborately carved timber beams and an enormous metal cooking pot.

Calle Salvatierra runs down towards the waterfront, where the Hotel Misión can be found. Beyond it is the fishing pier and Alfredo's tourist office. At the other end of the waterfront, four blocks south, is the Hotel Oasis, standing in its own grounds. At all of these you can book fishing trips or hire a boat to visit **Isla del Carmen**, with its solar salt works, or the tiny **Coronado** island only a mile offshore. Marlin swim up the gulf and arrive in quantity in mid-May and grouper, sailfish and many other species also flourish here.

Loreto was Baja's first capital, and remained so for 132 years, until, after a disastrous hurricane in 1828, the capital was moved to La Paz. In 1877 a major earthquake destroyed much of what remained of Loreto, and between then and 1959, when it was devastated by another earthquake, it was plagued again and again by pirate raids, floods and other disasters.

Completion of the Trans-Peninsula Highway, and the building of a new air strip has increased tourism, which is expected to boom with the completion of a new marina and Fonatur's major resort at **Nopolo**, some 8km (5 miles) south of Loreto. This ambitious government project will include golf courses, a tennis center and several hotels, one of which, now called the Radisson, has been operating as a self-contained resort for some years already.

Thirty-seven kilometers (23 miles) southwest along a steep mountain road, through magnificent scenery, is the beautifully preserved **San Javier mission**; the drive takes about two hours. The splendid mission, which is still in use as a church, was originally built in 1699 by Salvatierra's assistant Padre Francisco Piccolo, abandoned after Indian attacks, then reopened by Father Ugarte, who, having learned the Cochimi language, induced the Indians to return.

San Javier mission is still in use

The historian Clavigera said Ugarte had 'a strong constitution, extraordinary physical strength, a sublime mind, a natural penetrating talent, which was quick and facile for all the sciences and the arts, rare industry and prudence in economic affairs, and a heroic magnanimity superior to all obstacles and dangers.' The Indians were even more impressed by the fact that when they met a lion on a mountain trail one day Ugarte threw stones to bring it down and then choked it to death with his bare hands. Up until then the Indians had believed that to kill a mountain lion was to court their own imminent death. Ugarte roasted this one, and they ate it for their dinner.

When Ugarte died in 1730 he was buried at the mission where he had labored so valiantly. His successor, Miguel del Bareco, rebuilt the mission, which is generally regarded as the finest architectural example of its type in Baja. The village of **San Javier** is a pleasant little place with one restaurant but no hotel. Self-described 'out of shape' cyclist Peter Harmon of Washington, DC, cycled there from Loreto, a stiff climb that took him five hours. After that, although mostly downhill on a rough road, it took him a full day to reach Highway 1 at Santo Domingo.

7. Loreto to La Paz

—Most of the visitors to this area and all the way down to the peninula's southern tip, fly in to the commercial airports at La Paz or San José del Cabo. Loreto to La Paz is 354km (220 miles).—

Enticing beaches and the reddish-brown slopes of the Sierra de la Giganta make for spectacular scenery south of Loreto. The coastal highway is notable for dangerous curves and switchbacks before the road heads inland traversing a wide valley, a major farming region where oases of green land speckle the Magdalena Plain.

Twenty-five kilometers (16 miles) south of Loreto, a new resort is being created at **Puerto Escondido** in a beautiful bay, and you may consider it worth the short detour.

At Ciudad Constitución, Highway 22 heads 58km (36 miles) west to the port of **San Carlos**, a small town overlooking mango-fringed Bahía Magdalena which shelters a commercial fishing fleet and where whales can sometimes be seen.

Agricultural worker

Ciudad Constitución, looking something like a town out of the old American West, is a fast-growing (pop: 45,000) busy agricultural center which produces cotton, wheat, and vegetables. Almost all of the area's water supply comes from wells, making it possible for such an arid place to be so productive. Men and boys on horseback can be seen along the main street. It is not a tourist town although it does have hotels, trailer parks, a supermarket and an interesting public market. The best place for a meal or stopover is at the Hotel Maribel (on the highway) which has a restaurant called Sancho Panza which serves good Mexican-style food.

Fourteen kilometers (9 miles) south of the town an unpaved road, signposted Presa El Thuayil, leads 50km (31 miles) southeast through an arid wasteland to an oasis in the desert housing the mission of **San Luis Gonzaga,** recently repaired by the National Institute of Anthropology and History. German Jesuit Lambert Hostell, who took charge of the mission in 1737, described the area as 'a land savage, rough, dry and unproductive throughout' and its inhabitants as 'a barbarous nation, brown in color, who pierce their ears and noses.'

Padre Johann Jakob Baegert, who took over in 1751, was one of the few missionaries to write extensively. 'The native Californians seem to thrive on anything. For them this is the most delightful place on the face of the earth... One might consider them the poorest and most pitiable of God's children yet I will state without fear of contradiction that, as far as this earthly life is concerned, they are incomparably happier than those who live in Europe. A native Californian sleeps as gently and

San Luis Gonzaga mission

as well on the hard earth under the open sky as any European in his soft, feather bed... These Californians seem to have nothing yet at all times they have what they need.'

Constructed of bright rose-colored stone, the mission stands beside a lagoon bordered with date palms. Baegert wrote that the Indians learned stone masonry and brick laying while building the mission. Scaffolding was made from poles tied together with rawhide or the bark of palm trees. As was common in desert regions where wood was short, shrubs and stalks of mescal plants were used to fire the kiln to make adobe bricks for building.

The village surrounding a typical mission would include a church, parsonage, storehouse, soldiers' dwellings, a school, and sometimes houses for neophytes, although in remoter regions the Indians followed their usual custom of living outdoors. Selected children were taught music in school: the harp, the violin, etc, and also taught to sing in the choir. After breakfast of *pozoli* (corn mush) the Indians went out to work in the fields, returning for a lunch of meat or fruit. Work in the afternoons, an evening meal and prayers ended the day. Looms were installed, and cotton was grown in some places, but much clothing also had to be brought from Mexico City. Each mission was more or less self-sufficient so those with good herds or abundant crops were richer than others. The mission was closed in 1769. Nearby is the green-gold mansion of Don Benigna de la Toba, a cattle baron who owned most of this area in the mid 19th century.

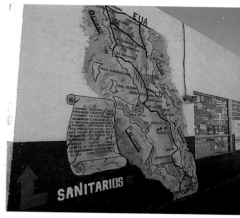

When you return to the main road, there is a completely straight stretch through flat land to the village of **Santa Rita**. From here an unpaved road runs eastwards through Agua de los Coyotes and several other communities, including San José del Zapote, to reach the gulf coast at the fishing village of **San Evaristo**, a distance of 170km (80 miles). Another route to this destination is from La Paz, heading north on the paved road to San Juan de la Costa and then on the dirt road past Punta Mechudo to San Evaristo (*mechudo* means 'hairy' – a good description of the cliffside section at Punta Mechudo). The channel between the coast and Isla San José here is highly favored by fishermen.

La Paz (pop: 180,000) became the capital of Baja in 1830 and until early this century had steamboat connections to other Baja ports. There are now daily ferries to the Mexican mainland. The ferry ticket office is on the corner of 5 de Mayo and Guillermo Pieto;

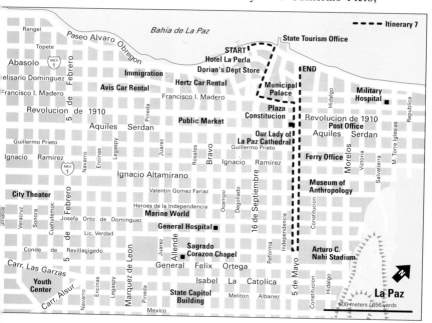

Walking on the waterfront

the terminal is in Pichilingue, to the north of the town. Famous for its gorgeous sunsets, it is a delightful town, its streets shaded by coconut palms and laurel trees. Jacaranda, acacia and flame trees make a colorful street display in spring. Late summer is the rainy season when *chubascos* (brief, sudden tropical storms) are expected.

Visited by Ferdinand Magellan in 1521 who was searching for a safe haven for the homeward-bound galleons from the Orient, La Paz was the unlucky recipient of a visit from the maverick adventurer William Walker who, in 1853, sailed in with 300 men from San Francisco, hauling down the Mexican flag and replacing it with his own. The Mexicans sent a defense force to regain their town and Walker, by now in San Diego meeting with co-conspirators, was arrested for breaching neutrality laws, although he was later released. Two years later, after a similar buccaneering adventure in Honduras, he was captured and executed.

Sign at El Quinta Sol

The favored stopping place in La Paz is the delightful Hotel Perla, on the **Paseo Obregón**, known as the *malecón* (waterfront), near the **tourist office** (tel: 2-59-39). Its terrace restaurant is a major gathering spot in late afternoon to drink and watch the sunset. From here it will take you about two hours to see the main places in town. Walk two blocks along the *malecón* past the tourist office (tel. 2-5939) and up 16 de Septiembre, passing the shopping mall anchored by Dorian's department store. Opposite is the **Municipal Palace,** once the Governor's Palace, with some interesting murals. This is the heart of the city's miniscule Chinatown and also the site of its best known vegetarian restaurant,

54

El Quinta Sol (junction of Dominguez and Independencia streets).

At Madero, turn left and walk two blocks to the **Zócalo**, or **Plaza Constitución**, as it's called here. The mission which stood here was abandoned in 1749; the city's cathedral, with twin pink-stone belltowers now stands on the site. Look inside the **biblioteca** which has some English-language history books in a glass-fronted case. An exhibition of paintings includes one of the legendary Indian queen Calafia; other pictures depict Salvatierra's mission in Loreto and Hernán Cortés' visit on May 3, 1533. Cortés arrived here with three ships and 500 men after earlier visitors had reported on the rich pearls to be found. The colonists remained for two years. La Paz, which means peace, was so named because the early visitors reported that the Indians were peaceful.

The library also contains a gruesome depiction of a Spanish soldier with an arrow through his throat after he was caught trying to rape Indian women and loot pearls. There are also attractive color photos of beaches, and photographs of Erle Stanley Gardner and whaler Charles Melville Scammon (see *Itinerary 3*, pages 32–37). There are cinemas just behind the library and also on Revolución, just off the Zócalo.

Four blocks south along Revolución at Degollado is a busy **covered market** (mostly food and clothing) but for now we'll continue up 5 de Mayo past the Sematur office (ferry boat tickets) to Altamirano. Here the **Museum of Anthropology** (Tuesday to Saturday, 9am–6pm; donation) features early geological finds, including a skeleton or two, and a garish, life-size mural of extinct animals. To the rear is a sculpture garden dominated by a big, brightly colored Aztec calendar wheel. A section titled *Imaginación Fantástico* needs no translation and includes masks and strange feathered figures of the type Indians still make today. The top floor is the most interesting being the recreated room of a typical Baja rancher of a century ago: there are skins covering a bare, mud floor, carved chests containing belongings, and a display of kitchen utensils.

Further up 5 de Mayo is the sports stadium, opposite which is the town's laundromat (7am–9pm weekdays, 9am–3pm Sundays). About a mile south along Ignacio Altamirano is the architecturally interesting **Teatro del Ciudad** (tel: 5-02-07) which also includes a gallery, a children's park and an open-air theater. It is well worth the walk if you avoid the fiercest heat of the day. For those who are not traveling by car, the long-distance **bus station** (tel: 2-42-70) is out this way at Jalisco and Independencia, an inexpensive taxi ride from downtown or

Mayan sculpture

via any bus headed for the downtown market. Local buses go from the terminal at Degollado and Revolución, and from the bus station on Obregón, just opposite the tourist office. That's pretty much all there is to La Paz, and most of your remaining time will probably be spent around the seafront. Walk back down 5 de Mayo and have lunch at the Oasis.

Northwards out of La Paz a good road goes up the Magote peninsula to Pichilingue (an hourly bus continues out to the beaches) passing the desalinization plant and through **Coromuel** (named after an English pirate named Cromwell) with its beach and restaurant. Pirate treasure is said to have been buried there but nobody has found it yet. Coromuel (which is the name of one of the Sematur ferries, as well) also means 'breeze' in Spanish. There is a beach called El Tesoro (treasure), 13km (8 miles) from town, with a restaurant. At **Pichilingue**, on the hillside opposite the ferry dock, is the Restaurant Bellavista and just up the road and around a bend is another nice little beach. Pichilingue is derived from the name

The beach at Tecolote

given to the Dutch pirates. There are even better beaches in lovely bays at **Balandra** and **Tecolote** at the end of the peninsula, past the commercial port at which most of the goods for Baja Sur are landed, and the whole area is also good for water sports.

Eight kilometers (5 miles) offshore in the gulf are the volcanic islands which partly shelter the southern portion of the vast Bahía de la Paz. These islands are the tiny

Partida, and 22-km (14-mile) long **Espíritu Santo** (Holy Spirit) with its 610-m (2,000-ft) high mesa, once known as the *isla de perlas*, after Cortés harvested black pearls there. A French company tried, unsuccessfully, to revive the industry earlier this century but the island is now uninhabited.

Pearls may now be in short supply in the Bahía de la Paz, but shark and shrimp fishing are very popular. There are daily boat tours to some of the nearby islands, where you can be almost guaranteed to see pelicans, sea lions and dolphins. **Isla de Cerralvo**, off the coast south of La Paz, is the southernmost island in the Sea of Cortés. Twenty-six kilometers (16 miles) by 7km (4 miles) in size, it has been uninhabited since the 1940s when the oysters which provided the islanders with their sole means of livelihood were wiped out by a mysterious disease.

8. La Paz to Los Cabos

—Cabo San Lucas is larger and more popular but San José del Cabo is older and more interesting; the latter has style and history, the former bulges with bars, cafes and night spots. Via Highway 1, it is 219km (136 miles) from La Paz to San José del Cabo.—

Roadside grazing

Highway 1 out of La Paz turns southeast just below San Pedro (where Highway 19 branches off towards Cabo San Lucas via Todos Santos). Just beyond the junction on Highway 1 is **El Triunfo** where silver was discovered in 1748. A church was built in 1825 and half a century later the village had a population of 10,000 — mostly Yaqui Indians from Sonora — and was shipping $50,000-worth of silver each month. The mine was abandoned in 1918 and there is little happening in El Triunfo now, but it is a picturesque little village.

Los Barriles is a fast-growing little town on the coast, with a couple of hotels, some shops and cafes, and sometimes sport-fishing boats for rent. From here, a passable dirt road heads unevenly for about 160km (100 miles) around the entire cape to San José del Cabo, passing tiny fishing communities, camping spots and beaches empty except for windsurfers and snorkelers.

There's a zoo in Santiago (some 25km/15 miles) from Los Barriles), specializing in indigenous animals and birds. **Santiago** is a pleasant agricultural community although all traces of the mission established here in 1724 have disappeared. A revolt by the Pericu Indians began here with the murder of Padre Carranco and epidemics later wiped out most of the Indian population, causing the mission to be abandoned in 1795. Nearby is **Miraflores** which is famous for its fine leather work and its cheeses.

El Triunfo's church

There are many *cabos* (capes) at Baja's southern tip but two – Cabo San Lucas and San José del Cabo – have become famous, and the 32-km (20-mile) coastal corridor between them is filling up with glossy resort hotels. Originally renowned for sport fishing, the Cabos have become places for luxurious vacations under the transforming hands of Fonatur, the government development organization. It is sunny every day of the year and its high season is from November to May when it is not too hot. The climate is tropical in summer and fall, which is also the superior fishing time.

The region is rich with sugar cane, papayas, mangoes and bananas, and the waters teem with fish. The spongy-looking backscratchers called loofahs, which look like sea creatures, actually grow on vines in the Cabos region. They are the fibrous interior of a dry fruit which is originally green but gradually loses its color.

Thirteen kilometers (8 miles) north of San José is the international airport. At **San José del Cabo**, (pop: 22,000) before Highway 1 skirts the west side of town, make a left turn on Zaragoza which leads to the main street, **Boulevard Mijares**. At the top of this street are the **city hall**, **the plaza** and the twin-towered **San José church**, built in 1940 on the site of the 18th-century mission. Above the door is a mosaic depicting Padre Nicolás Tamaral's murder by the Indians.

Further down the hill are the official buildings: **post office**, **police station** and **fire department**. In these two blocks can also be found a shopping mall, the attractive Tropicana Inn, some good eating places and the unmistakable Iguana Bar which has a dance

Killer Hook Surf Shop

floor and nightly entertainment. One block over on Hidalgo is the inexpensive Hotel Colli and the adjoining Cafeteria Girasol as well as the Killer Hook Surf Shop, run by affable Rafael Green and his lovely wife Cleo, from whom you can rent surfboards, snorkeling gear or surfing videos. Rafael, a fifth generation Josefino, promises that he can answer virtually any question about Cabo that comes to your mind.

A few blocks west of the plaza, between Coronado and Castro, is the **municipal market** with innumerable stalls offering cheap food. Nearby is the bus station. When you have explored the town – it won't take long – rent a bicycle (ask Rafael), walk or take a taxi along Juarez from opposite the fire station, and head past the groves of mangoes, papayas and guavas towards **La Playita**. At this lovely, windswept beach you can rent *pangas* (skiffs) in which to go fishing, or – in season – head out for some whale-watching. You'll pass two simple restaurants on the way, both offering ex-

Hotel Presidente beach

cellent seafood. You can follow the beach right round past the estuary to the Hotel Presidente and then walk back up into town from there. The Boulevard Paseo San José runs along the shore passing four big hotels and a shopping market, **Plaza Los Cabos**, before rejoining Highway 1.

The **estuary,** where an underground river surfaces, is home to 200 species of birds, and rumors of an impending marina are not being welcomed by everybody in town. The original 1730 mission was on the beach west of the estuary but in 1753 it was rebuilt at its present site overlooking the plaza. In those days San José was a refitting port for treasure-laden galleons on their 8-month journey from Manila to Spain. Exploring Baja by mule in 1868, the Irishman John Ross Brown wrote of San José: 'The native citizens are lazy and harmless, devoting themselves chiefly to sleeping and gambling.'

Separated from the highway only by a few hundred yards of sandhills studded with bush and cactus, the turquoise sea washes pristine beaches along the 32-km (20-mile) corridor that separates the two Cabos. The charming **Hotel Palmilla**, ablaze with colorful oleander and bougainvillea, on the highway 7km (4 miles) west of San José, was the first hotel in these parts, opened almost half a century ago. Bing Crosby, Frank Sinatra, John Wayne and Dwight Eisenhower were frequent visitors. At the hotel, you can arrange snorkeling trips, play golf on an excellent course, or rent horses for riding (or you can just enjoy the entertainment in the bar). The adjoining beach is one of the safest in an area which is mostly not ideal for swimming because of rough seas and a strong undertow. The government began to develop this area for tourism in the 1980s and there are now 200,000 visitors a year. The Regine Western Hotel is a luxurious venue which caters to some of them, and the numbers will continue to grow.

Chapel at Hotel Palmilla

Keeping cool in the Cabos

Between the two capes overlooking **Chileno Bay** on a spectacular headland is the luxurious Hotel Cabo San Lucas, with Aztec fountains set in its 1,012-ha (2,500-acre) grounds. Between the plush hotels you will occasionally see a bulldozer sitting in freshly cleared ground, and shiny billboards evoke such names as Jack Nicklaus and Robert Trent Jones as promise of golf courses to come. There are ambitious plans for two additional resort projects – Cabo Real and Cabo del Sol – with all the usual facilities: thousands of hotel rooms, golf courses, condominiums, tennis courts, a marina and yacht club.

Cabo San Lucas (pop: 20,000), a favorite hiding place for 17th-century pirates who lay in wait to ambush Spanish treasure ships, is now a popular stop-off for cruise ships. It is an enormously popular refuge for fishermen and for younger tourists who are drawn to the lively nightlife, most of which is found around Boulevard Cárdenas and Marina, near the **marina** itself. Almost all the non-hotel action, day or night, takes place around the **flower-filled plaza** or the nearby marina. You can drink and dance until late at the Corona Beach Club, El Squid Roe, the rock star-owned Cabo Wabo Cantina, or at the cavernous Giggling Marlin, where zaniness is encouraged.

From the marina you can take a glass-bottomed boat trip to see the tropical fish (scuba gear can be rented), occasional sea lions and the distinctive rock **Los Arcos** which marks land's end. The excursion passes the secluded **Lovers' Beach**, where the waves from the gulf and the ocean collide dramatically against each other. Boats will drop you off and pick you up from Lovers' Beach (where the

Dropping off at Lovers' Beach

surf sometimes gets dangerously high), but you can walk to it round the coast in half an hour. Closer to town is the beach beside the Hacienda Hotel which has calmer waves. For waterskiing, windsurfing and for lunch, the most popular beach is **Medano** from which whale-watching tours depart between January and April. These waters are also ideal for scuba diving, and all the necessary gear can be rented. It is also ideal for swimming, of course.

Visit the site of the **old lighthouse**, 8km (5 miles) west at Cabo Falso (once believed to be the southernmost point) to see the view. Three-hour tours in four-wheel-drive vehicles are available. Only the frame of the lighthouse remains, as the 1890 structure was destroyed in a 1957 storm. The bus station is at the junction of Zaragoza and 16 de Septiembre (tel: 684/3-04-00).

Westwards out of Cabo San Lucas the highway follows the coast on the way back to La Paz, passing through **Todos Santos**, set in a tropical region (it stands exactly on the Tropic of Cancer) and renowned for its mangoes and sugar cane. In winter-time a dark candy called *panocha* is made at the local sugar mill. The mission founded here by Padre Tamaral in 1733 was destroyed during the Indian rebellion of the following year. It had been named in honor of Doña Rosa de la Pena, sister-in-law of the Marques de Villa-puente, who had contributed 10,000 pesos for its support.

Picturesque Hotel California

The wealthy Villapuente, who donated over half a million acres of land over the years, financing such missions as San José del Cabo, Comondú, Purísima, Guadalupe and Santa Gertrudis, probably had a better idea than most of the frustrations of the missionaries. One letter he received from Taraval described attempts to introduce monogamy to the Indians as 'the most invisible obstacle.' It benefited the men to have numerous wives, the padre said, because 'the greater the number of wives the so much better are they served and provided with all necessities.

'They recline in perpetual idleness in the shade of the trees, and their wives work hunting in the woods for wild roots and fruits... trying to take the best that she finds to the husband to win his affection above his other wives.' About 1,000 Indians perished here in a 1742 epidemic and the original mission is now a pile of stones about a mile from town. The church, built on the present site in 1840, was destroyed by a hurricane a century later, then rebuilt.

The **Hotel California** on Calle Juarez y Márquez de León, with a pool and restaurant, organizes guided pack trips into the nearby **sierras.** The town is half a mile inland from some lovely, lonely beaches, but the ocean is rough.

Shopping

Baja is not an ideal place to shop for distinctive goods, but it is great for bargains. Most shops display the usual souvenir-type goods, including hats, jewelry and woven items that can be found anywhere else in Mexico. Exceptions to this generalization are to be found in the larger towns of Ensenada and, especially, Tijuana, which is often described as a shopper's paradise. And if you need your hair cut, your shoes mended or your car repaired, Tijuana offers all these services at competitive prices.

Local leather goods

Tijuana is a duty free port, like all of Baja, and as such it offers both Mexican handicrafts and imported goods at much lower prices than apply in the United States. The greatest variety of stores is on Avenida Revolución, the main street in town, where the Casa de Mexico and the Government Store, among others, sell authentic Mexican handicrafts. Other shops on this street offer a range of goods from Cuban cigars to Italian fashions, French perfumes to Spanish leatherwork, all at temptingly low, duty-free prices.

The Mercado Artesianas, on 2nd Street near the Mexitlan complex, is a good place to look for arts and crafts, and the Plaza Rio Tijuana shopping mall, which stays open until 9pm, is the largest shopping center in northwest Mexico with approximately 100 stores offering bargains and great opportunities for browsing to your heart's content. The area around Agua Caliente Racetrack is also a shopper's delight and includes the Plaza Patria mall which specializes in shoes. In most places you will find the usual collections of T-shirts, sombreros and pottery donkeys that you would expect in a town that caters to tourists, but there are also good quality items to be had as well if you search around.

Gifts from San José del Cabo

Ensenada's prices are often even lower than Tijuana's. Next to the State Tourist Office on Avenida López Mateos is the Fonart Government Store which specializes in fixed-priced Mexican crafts. Check out the craft stores around Avenida Castillo and Boulevard Lázaro Cárdenas (also known as Boulevard Costero). The latter has a huge commercial craft market, the Centro Artesanal.

South of Ensenada there is very little of interest to buy. Craftware is almost non-existent and shops aimed at tourists sell pretty much the same kitsch as can be found anywhere, although there are some exceptions. One is **Loreto**, where the souvenir shop across from the mission has some interesting, low-priced items; and Originales de Mexico and Bazar Moctezuma Miscelaneos also offer quite a few ethnic bargains.

In **La Paz** there are souvenir shops along the *malecón* and behind the Hotel Perla, whose next-door neighbor, appropriately, sells pearls, the commodity on which the town was founded. There is also the block-long department store along Constitución, which is like a giant US drugstore.

Centro Commercial Plaza in **Cabo San Lucas** has shops selling clothing, jewelry and woven goods; and Mama Eli's Curios nearby has some items worth noting. The marina market is interesting but touristy, and has a good display of onyx elephants and attractive glass miniatures of whales and seals. If you love gold and silver, go to the store in the Hotel Meliá on El Medano street to see its selection.

In **San José del Cabo** wander around Zaragoza and Mijares to find hand-painted clothes, crafts and folk art.

An original use for coconuts

Eating Out

Seafood, as you would expect, is one of the culinary delights of the Baja peninsula. Most places detailed in this book's itineraries are on the coast, or quite close to it. You'll find lobster widely available but surprisingly expensive. San Felipe's *malecón* is lined with seafood stalls, which are a good idea for a quick snack, and those of La Paz are especially recommended as they are regularly inspected by health officials. A good one is Culiacán (Serdan near Marquez de León) whose wide range of dishes includes octopus, shrimp and oysters but whose specialty is the *almejas rellenas* (stuffed clams). Another good choice is Mariscos Balamar (5 de Febrero at Yucatán). (*Mariscos* means shellfish, and is a word you will find on many menus.)

Tijuana, in particular, has some excellent restaurants at affordable prices, many of them with tables on shady terraces and patios. The most elegant is the Place de la Concorde on Boulevard Agua Caliente, which specializes in French cuisine, but there are many other good ones with an authentic Mexican atmosphere. The following is a list of recommended restaurants.

$ = under $5 (per person); $$ = $5–10; $$$ = over $10.

Tropicana Inn, San José del Cabo

Cabo San Lucas

RESTAURANT DELFIN
Playa Médano
Right on the beach. $$

COCONUTS
Cascadas de Baja
East of town
Tel: 3-03-7
Tiled floors and graceful archways, it calls itself 'the most romantic restaurant.' $$

THE GIGGLING MARLIN
Matamoros at Marina
Tel: 3-06-06
Lively bar with lots of dancing, fun and games. $$

The Giggling Marlin

SEÑOR SUSHI'S
Opposite Plaza Las Glorias
Tel: 3-13-23
'Everything but sushi' includes lobster, steak ribs, chicken. $$

LA TERRAZA
At the marina
Wide selection, sushi to pizza; eating outdoors. $

SHOOTERZ
Madero & Guerrero
Mexican and American cuisine. $$

PAPPI'S
Zaragoza
A Mexican deli with burgers and ice cream. $

KAN KUN
Adjoining Hotel Marina
Casual place for big breakfasts to start the day. $

PIZZA OCEANO
Lázaro Cárdenas
Tel: 3-09-31
A favorite with locals. A variety of Italian food as well as pizza. $

SHRIMP FACTORY
Blvd Marina
Tel: 3-11-47
A bucket is enough for four. $$

Ensenada

LA CASA DEL ABULON
Blvd Costero
Tel: 6-57-85
Great seafood and ocean views. $$$

LAS CAZUELAS
Boulevard Sangines 6
Tel: 6-10-44
Try the abalone with lobster sauce. $$$

CHINA LAND
Av Riveroll 1149
Tel: 8-86-44
More than 100 Asian dishes. $$

SEÑOR SALUD
9th Espinoza Street
Tel: 6-44-15
Vegetarian dishes. $$

LA FLOR DE ITALIA
Av Ruiz 96
Tel: 8-12-20
As Italian as it sounds. $$

La Paz

RESTAURANT DRAGON
16 de Septiembre and Esquerro
Tel: 2-13-72
Upstairs, open late; casual ambiance.
$$

OASIS
Opposite tourist office on Obregón
Tel: 5-76-66
Dining betwixt the trees. Vast menu,
open late. $$

LA TERRAZA
Obregón 1570
Tel: 2-07-77
Hotel Perla's sidewalk hang-out op-
posite the *malecón*. The best place to
watch the sunset. $$

RESTAURANT BERMEJO
Hotel Los Arcos
Malecón
Tel: 2-27-44
Seafood, steak and Mexican-style food.
$$

BISMARK II
Altamirano and Degollado
Tel: 2-48-54
First-class seafood. $$

EL TASTE
Malecón, just past Los Arcos
Tel: 2-81-21
'Famous for lobster.' $$

ROSTICCERIA CALIFORNIA
Serdan and Bravo
Restaurant and take-away counter, siz-
zling roast chicken sold complete or by
the piece. $

PALAPA ADRIANA
Malecón at Hidalgo
Tel: 2-33-29
Inexpensive beach restaurant with
thatched roof. $

EL MOLINO STEAKHOUSE
Beside the marina, Bahía de la Paz
Tel: 2-98-96
Seafood as well as mouth-watering
steaks. $$

LA CALETA
*On the malecón two blocks north of
Los Arcos*
Beach restaurant and bar. $

Good and generous

Loreto

CESAR'S
Juárez at Zapata
Tel: 3-02-03
Loreto's oldest and probably best
restaurant. Good food, occasional mu-
sical entertainment. $$$

EL NIDO
Salvatierra 154
Opposite the bus station
Tel: 3-02-84
Atmosphere is fishnets, oak beams and
open fireplace/grill. Good food,
mostly steak and seafood. $$

PLAYA BLANCA
Hidalgo and Davis
Bright, cheerful upstairs room over-
looks the street. Varied menu. $$

CAFE OLÉ
Madero
Tel: 3-04-96
Just off the plaza. Perfect for break-
fast and people-watching. $

TIFFANY'S PIZZA
Opposite Hotel Plaza on Hidalgo
Tel: 3-05-97
Italian-American owner who is very proud of his product. $

HOTEL MISION RESTAURANT
Beside the hotel's swimming pool on the malecón
Tel: 3-00-48
Open all day. Ample menu, comparable prices. $$

EL EMBARCADERO
Boulevard Mateos, opposite the fishing harbor
Tel: 3-10-65
The owner operates the adjoining fishing tackle store so fresh fish is a specialty. $$

Mexicali

LA CASITA DE PATZCUA
Boulevard López Mateos
Tel: 52-97-07
Small, centrally located. $$

SANBORNS
Calzada Independencia
Tel: 57-52-62
One of the old, familiar chain. $$

CHALET
Calzado Justo Sierra 889
Tel: 68-20-01
Tasty international cuisine. $$$

MISION DRAGON
Boulevard Lázaro Cárdenas
Tel: 66-43-75; 66-44-00
Beautifully decorated Chinese place. $$$

RIVOLI
Boulevard Benito Juárez 2151
Tel: 66-10-00
Good quality food, with plenty of choice. $$$

Mulegé

LOS EQUIPALES
Moctezuma near Zaragoza
Tel: 3-03-30
Cool airy terrace upstairs. Spotless and attractive with soft music. $$

EL NIDO
Calle Rubio, near the river
Tel: 3-02-21
Steaks, fish and chicken. $$

POLLO SALVATE (The Wild Chicken)
Zaragoza, just north of the square
Hole in the wall snackery. $

El Almeja restaurant

EL ALMEJA RESTAUARANT
North side of the river
Delightful beachside restaurant with amicable owner. $

LAS CASITAS
Hotel Las Casitas
Callejón de los Estudiantes
Tel: 3-00-19
Seafood and Mexican mariachi band on Friday night. $$

LA JUNGLA BAMBU
South bank of river, ½-mile from town
Tel: 3-02-00
Outdoor dining under the trees. Big-screen Monday night football. $

EL CANDIL
Zaragoza
Down tiny passageway to tree-shaded patio. $$

San José del Cabo

LE BISTRO
Morelos 4
Tel: 2-11-74
French chef, outdoor tables, crepes, bouillabaisse. $$

SANDRICK'S HAMBURGERS
Boulevard Mijares 28, upstairs
Mexican/American cooking in full view. $

DIANA'S
Zaragoza 30
Tel: 2-04-90
Tables on open terrace; good margaritas. $

CAFE EUROPA
Boulevard Mijares
Tel: 2-12-18
Tasty European cuisine, good coffee. $$

IVAN'S EUROPEAN RESTAURANT
Boulevard Mijares, opposite City Hall
Great breakfasts, Greek salads, free champagne with dinner. $$

IGUANA BAR
Boulevard Mijares 24
Tel: 2-02-66
Satellite sports TV. $

DAMIAN'S
Boulevard Mijares, near the plaza
Tel: 2-04-99
In 18th-century hacienda, open till midnight. $$

The popular Iguana Bar

DA GIORGIO
Highway 1, west of town, near Hotel Palmilla
Good Italian food. $$

Tijuana

ALCAZAR DEL RIO
Paseo de los Héroes
Tel: 84-26-72
International menu. $$$

BOCCACCIO
Boulevard Agua Caliente
Tel: 86-22-66
Seafood and steaks. $$$

LA ESCONDIDA
Las Palmas Avenue
Tel: 81-44-58
A locals' favorite. Serves enormous margaritas. $$$

HACIENDA DEL ABAJEÑO
Sanchez Taboa and Antonio Caso
Tel: 84-27-91
Mexican folk music in a fountain-filled patio. $$$

GUADALAJARA BAR & GRILL
Calle Orozco and Paseo de los Héroes
Mexican street scene setting. $$

PLACE DE LA CONCORDE
Fiesta Americana Hotel, Boulevard Agua Caliente
Tel: 81-70-00
Tijuana's most elegant restaurant, with excellent French cuisine. $$$

LA PLACITA
Avenida Revolución 783
Tel: 88-27-04
Moderately priced, with music. $$

TOUR DE FRANCE
Gobernador Ibarra and Highway 1
Tel: 81-75-42
Patio, French food. $$

Calendar of Special Events

JANUARY / FEBRUARY

January 6 Día de los Reyes (The Day of the Kings): the traditional day for exchanging Christmas gifts. Processions of the Kings are held in some local towns.

January 21 International Canofila Exposition, Mexicali.

February 11 San Felipe carnival.

February 18 Grand Prix, held annually in Mexicali.

mid-February The week preceding Ash Wednesday is Lenten carnival week, known as Carnaval. Colorful celebrations, with dances, processions and loud music.

MARCH / APRIL

March 19 Festival of St Joseph, held in San José del Cabo as he is the town's patron saint.

April Easter Week celebrations.

April 16 Rosarito to Ensenada race by bicycle.

April 30 Tijuana pizza festival.

MAY / JUNE

May 1 Labor Day (Día del Trabajo)

May 22 Exciting Tecate to Ensenada race by bicycle.

May 22 Rodeo in Tecate.

early-June (first Thursday) Corpus Christi.

June 21 Fiesta at San Luis Gonzaga. Mission was closed in 1768 but a small stone church remains dating from the 1750s.

June 24 Festival of St John (locally, San Juan).

Dressed for the fiesta

September 4 Santa Rosalia fiesta at this town and Mulegé.

September 8 La Virgen de Loreto: a colorful procession through the streets carrying the image of the virgin from the mission is preceded by eight days of preparatory visits to local homes.

September 15–16 Independence Day celebrations.

October Annual Lobster and Wine Festival, Rosarito.

October Annual Bisbee Black and Blue Marlin fishing tournament held in Los Cabos.

October 12 Columbus Day (locally, Día de la Raza).

Oct 30 San Francisco de Borja: fiesta centered around the old church and ruined mission.

JULY / AUGUST

July (dates vary) Harvest festival at Guadalupe Valley wineries located near Tecate.

July (dates vary) Annual Ensenada exposition has industrial and agricultural exhibits, as well as a variety of food displays.

July 25 The saint's day of Santiago Apóstol is celebrated at Santiago, south of La Paz.

July 31 San Ignacio Loyola: colorful fiesta in San Ignacio for its patron saint's day.

August La Pamplonada: the running of the bulls through and around the streets of Tecate.

August Guadalupe Valley Wine Festival, dates vary.

August Todos Santos (south of Ensenada) annual regatta.

SEPTEMBER / OCTOBER

September Rosarito-Ensenada 50-Mile Fun Bicycle Ride.

September Annual International Seafood Fair, Ensenada.

NOVEMBER / DECEMBER

November 1 All Saints' Day (Día de todos los Santos), also known as the Day of the Dead.

November 15 Santa Gertrudis: religious holiday on the town's patron saint's day, centered on the Dominican mission.

November Coast to coast event: Baja Peninsula off-road race.

A Baja buggy

December 3 San Javier festival celebrates the saint's day at the old mission near Loreto.

December 12 Festival of Virgin de Guadalupe in Guadalupe Valley and elsewhere in the area.

Practical Information

La Paz airport

Princess Cruises, 2020 Avenue of the Stars, Los Angeles, CA 90067 (tel: 213-553-1770).

Admiral Cruises, 1220 Biscayne Blvd, Miami, FL 33132 (tel: 800-331-1193).

Exploration Cruise Line, 1500 Metropolitan Park Bldg, Olive and Boren, Seattle, WA 98101.

TRAVEL ESSENTIALS

Climate

Temperatures are above 30°C (86°F) for most of the year, a little cooler between November and February. Rain is rare at all times of the year.

When to visit

As summer (March to October) is the hottest time, it is least comfortable for traveling. It is, however, the most favorable fishing season, and fine for swimming, scuba diving, etc, as long as you protect yourself against the sun's fierce rays.

Clothing

Light clothing is best almost all the time although nights in the desert and mountains can get very chilly and a warm sweater or jacket is important. Take cool and comfortable walking shoes also.

Visas

For visits of up to 72 hours, US and Canadian citizens can travel as far as Ensensada merely with some ID. South of Ensenada a tourist card is needed by everyone and

GETTING THERE

By air

Tijuana international airport, 10km (6 miles) east of downtown, is served by Aero California (tel: 800-237-6225); by Aeromexico (tel: 800-237-6639) and Mexicana (tel: 800-531-7921). Aeromexico also serves **Loreto** (tel: 3-02-05), **La Paz** (tel: 2-03-67) and **Los Cabos** (tel: 2-03-99). Mexicana also serves **La Paz** (tel: 2-43-89) and **Los Cabos** (tel: 2-06-06).

Air LA (tel: 800-933-5952) services **Tijuana** and has just begun daily flights from Los Angeles to **Mexicali**, and four-times-weekly flights to **San Felipe.** Alaska Airlines (tel: 800-426-0333) flies to **Los Cabos**, as does Mexicana and United Airlines (tel: 800-538-2929).

By boat

Starlite Cruises (tel: 800-488-7827) operates gambling cruises to Ensenada.

Western Cruise Lines, 140 W 6th St, San Pedro CA 90731 (tel: 800-772-7272).

a car permit is necessary if you are planning to take a car across to the Mexican mainland. These documents must be obtained before reaching the Baja port of exit. All non-US citizens should carry passports at all times.

Electricity

Just as north of the border, the voltage is 110 and the same plugs are used.

Time zone

The same as California in Baja Norte; California time is Pacific Standard from November to March and Pacific Daylight Time in summer. Baja Sur is one hour ahead in winter, but the same in summer.

Customs and Immigration

In addition to the usual prohibitions US Customs bans the import of pre-Columbian artifacts such as stone carvings or wall art works. Also readily available south of the border are such banned-from-the-US items as fireworks, onyx smoking pipes (considered to be 'drug paraphernalia'), certain martial arts weapons and switchblade knives.

GETTING ACQUAINTED

Geography / Population

The population of Baja California Norte is approaching 3 million, about half of which is in Tijuana and much of the rest in the two biggest cities, Mexicali (the capital) and Ensenada. The population of Baja Sur is around 300,000, about half of which is in La Paz (the capital).

A 'paseo' in La Paz

The entire Baja peninsula is almost 1,288km (800 miles) in length (1690km/ 1050 miles by road). A spine of mountains, mostly over 1,500m (5,000ft) runs down the center of the peninsula which ranges from 48 to 225km (30 to 140 miles) wide. On both coasts there are many natural bays and harbors and much of the interior – particularly in the central region – is desert with semi-tropical regions around Mulegé and the southern tip.

Money Matters

The devaluation of 1993 did everyone a favor by knocking three zeros off the inflated currency, although at present both the old notes and the new ones (they are identical except for denomination) circulate side by side and sometimes prices are still quoted in 'thousands' which is usually the old currency. The dollar sign ($) in Mexico invariably means pesos, often listed as N$, meaning 'new pesos' which have been stabilized at around three to the US dollar, although it varies by a few cents from day to day. In border areas, American currency is willingly accepted. Banks usually offer the best exchange rates and Banamex (Banco Nacional de Mexico), the largest, can be used to receive and send funds by wire. Traveler's checks can be cashed at banks and are accepted at some larger hotels and restaurants.

GETTING AROUND

By Car

For automobile drivers in Baja there is good news and bad news. The good news is that there is a good, major road – Mexico Highway 1 (the Trans-Peninsular Highway) – from the Tijuana border all the way down to the southern tip at Cabo San Lucas. It is fairly well maintained and for most of its length so unpopulated and uncrowded that you may go for miles without seeing another vehicle, except possibly long-distance trucks (whose drivers are invariably helpful and informed, and can use their CB radios to summon assistance if it is needed).

The bad news is that apart from Highway 2, connecting the border towns, and Highway 5, connecting Mexicali with the

east coast resort of San Felipe, there isn't much else. Or, to be accurate, there are hundreds of other roads but most of them are not only unsuitable for regular automobiles but are so far off the beaten track there isn't much chance of getting help in case of a breakdown. Still, there are always gamblers, and unsurfaced tracks all over Baja are festooned with the remains of cars whose owners found it cheaper to leave their vehicles behind than to pay for a 200-mile tow.

The Mexican government's much-vaunted Green Angels theoretically patrol all of the country's highways but are not highly visible in Baja itself.

However tempting an unpaved road might look it is usually better not to risk it unless you are in a truck or car with four-wheel-drive. Potholes are frequent enough, even on good roads, to keep you

constantly alert and on ungraded roads they are supplemented by other unexpected obstacles such as rocks, subsidence and the occasional cow. Be alert also for *vados*, sudden dips in the road, which are quite frequent on some highways. Back country roads will often be unmarked, disconcertingly leading to junctions that offer choices but no clues as to the correct route. The Automobile Club of Southern Califor`na's invaluable Baja California guide sensibly recommends that on these occasions it is better to choose the most-traveled route which at least will probably lead to a ranch where you can ask for more precise directions.

Gasoline, a government monopoly in Mexico, is sold in two grades: regular (leaded) gasoline dispensed from blue pumps and unleaded – known as *magna sin* – from green pumps. Pemex (Petróleos

Mexicanos) stations are frequent enough but not as widespread as in the US and *magna sin* is not available at every station. It is wise, therefore, to keep your tank topped up, especially as there are occasions when gas stations temporarily run out of supplies – especially over weekends and fiestas.

Check that the gasoline pumps register zero when the pumping begins, that the cap is replaced on the gasoline tank and give a peso to the boy who (unasked) cleans your windows.

Car permits are required in Baja only if drivers take their automobiles south of Ensenada or take them on the ferry across to the Mexico mainland. Proof of ownership is advisable, however. Permits (which are free) can be obtained at border cities and in Ensenada but not at ferry ports. It is mandatory to have Mexican car insurance when driving in Mexico because in case of an accident the car would otherwise be impounded until the case is settled – something that could take a long time. Both sides of the border are rife with insurance offices but it's a wise plan to join the Auto Club of Southern California, not only because they sell insurance but because of the additional one-stop help they can offer, including providing tourist and automobile permits, maps, route listings, etc.

Car Rentals

Auto rentals in Baja are expensive, much more so than in the United States, and few US companies allow their cars to be taken south of the border. One exception is Avis in San Diego which allows rental cars to be taken as far south as Guerrero Negro, but no further.

To rent a car from any of the following companies you should make reservations in advance.

Tijuana: Avis, Agua Caliente 3310, tel: 66/86-40-04

Budget, Paseo de los Héroes 77, tel: 66/84-02-53

National, Agua Caliente 5000, tel: 66/86-2103

Car rental companies have booths at all Baja airports.

Loreto: Budget, tel: 3-01-79
La Paz: Thrifty, tel: 5-96-96
Auto Rental Sol, tel: 2-27-44
Auto Renta, tel: 2-14-48
Cabo San Lucas: Hertz, tel: 3-02-11
Avis, tel: 3-07-76
San José del Cabo: Avis, tel: 800/70-777
National, tel: 2-04-04

Door-to-door service

Taxis

In Tijuana there are plenty of taxis as you end your walk across the border. Make sure you agree on a price for the (short) trip downtown. Taxis from the airport to downtown are about $10. In many towns such as Loreto, Mulegé, San Ignacio, La Paz, Guerrero Negro, where buses stop on the highway, taxis stand by to run visitors into town at a reasonable rate.

Buses

From the border, buses run to the bus station (tel: 66/86-9915) in downtown Tijuana at Calle 1a and Madero, but returning buses should be caught on Juarez between Revolución and Constitución. Information on long distance buses is available from Tijuana's Central de Autobuses (tel: 01152-66-86-9060) at Boulevards Lázaro Cárdenas and Alamar. Operating from there, Tres Estrellas de Oro and Autotransportes de Baja California (ABC) both run down to La Paz, a 24-hour trip. Information on bus schedules in other parts of Baja is not always reliable, so try to double-check.

The four main long-distance bus lines operate out of the central bus station, Camionera Central, on Avenida Independéncia.

HOURS AND HOLIDAYS

Business Hours

Banks and many other businesses open at 9am but close for lunch sometimes as early as noon, sometimes at 2pm, reopening again from 4–6pm.

In the larger towns, few shops now close at lunch time.

Public Holidays

January 1 New Year's Day
February 5 Constitution Day
February 24 Flag Day
March 19 Festival of St Joseph, San José del Cabo
March 21 Birthday of former president, Benito Juarez
April Easter Holy Week
May 1 Labor Day
May 5 Cinco de Mayo
June 1 Navy Day
September 15–16 Independence Day
October 12 Columbus Day
November 1–2 Day of the Dead
November 20 Anniversary of the Mexican Revolution
December 12 Festival of Our Lady of Guadalupe
December 25 Christmas Day

ACCOMMODATION

The following is a list of recommended hotels.
$ = up to $50 for a double room
$$ = $50–75
$$$ = $75–175

Bahía de los Angeles

VILLA VITA MOTEL
Reservations: 509 Ross Drive
Escondido CA 92025
Tel: (619) 298-4958
Central, opposite beach. Pool, restaurant, bar. $

Cabo San Lucas

CALINDA BEACH
Km 4.5 Trans-Peninsular Highway
Cabo San Lucas
Tel: (684) 3-00-44
Three pools, three hot tubs, tennis courts, great view of Los Arcos. $$$

HOTEL CABO SAN LUCAS
PO Box 48088
Los Angeles CA 90048
Tel: 800/SEE CABO
Outside town. Fountains and statuary dot the tropical gardens, private beach, hotel has airstrip. $$$

HOTEL FINISTERRA
Blvd Marina
On bluff south of town
Tel: (684) 3-00-00
Castle-on-a-cliff with beach, pool, top-notch restaurant. $$$

HOTEL SOLMAR
Blvd Marina, the furthest south
Tel: (684) 3-00-22
Secluded haven in cliffs. Pool, beach, tennis, etc. $$$

LOS CABOS INN
16 de Septiembre and Abasolo
Tel: (684) 3-05-10
Tiny motel just west of town. $

MAR DE CORTEZ
Calles Guerrero and Cárdenas
Tel: (684) 3-00-32
Downtown, near marina; pool, restaurant, bar. $

MELIA SAN LUCAS
Playa El Medano
Tel: (5) 596-2246
Enormous pool stretches almost to beach, two restaurants. $$$

Ensenada

BAHIA RESORT HOTEL
López Mateos and Alvarado
Tel: (667) 8-21-01
Midtown. Pool, ocean views, outdoor dining plus La Tortuga restaurant. $$

HOTEL PARAISO LAS PALMAS
Blvd Sagines 206
Tel: (526) 177-1701
Pool, jacuzzi, ocean view rooms. $$$

MOTEL AMERICA
López Mateos and Espinoza
Tel: 7-06-67
Popular with budget travelers. Back to back with Motel Sahara. $

MOTEL SAHARA
Calle Espinoza 174,
Tel: 6-02-07
Simple, clean, opposite the post office. $

Villa Fontana

VILLA FONTANA HOTEL
López Mateos 1050
Tel: (526) 678-3434
Stylish, two-story wooden building midtown, with pool, jacuzzi, stores. $$$

Guerrero Negro

EL MORRO MOTEL
Blvd Zapata
Tel: (685) 7-04-14
Just before town. Has restaurant. $

LAS DUNAS MOTEL
Blvd Zapata, adjoining market
No phone
Simple, rock-bottom cheap. $

La Paz

AQUARIO'S
Ramirez 1665 at Degollado
Tel: 2-92-66
Big concrete building with balconies; restaurant/bar. $$

CLUB EL MORRO HOTEL
Highway 11, northeast of town
Tel: (682) 2-40-84
Pleasant, with a shady garden. $$

HOSPEDAJE MARELI
Aquiles Serdan 283
Tel: (682) 2-10-17
Air-conditioned rooms behind a store at Bravo, six blocks from Zócalo. $

HOTEL PERLA
Paseo Obregón 1570
Tel: (682) 2-07-77
Irresistibly friendly place on the *malecón*. Popular restaurant, pool. $$

HOTEL PLAZA REAL
Esquerro and Callejón La Paz
Tel: (682) 2-93-33
Behind Hotel Perla. Clean, plain rooms, cafe. $

HOTEL POSADA SAN MIGUEL
Dominguez and 16 de Septiembre
Tel: (682) 2-18-02
Opposite Municipal Palace. Fan-cooled rooms around flower-filled courtyard. $

HOTEL PURISIMA
16 de Septiembre 408
Tel: (682) 2-34-44
Four floors of plain rooms overlooking busy downtown street. $

HOTEL YENEKA
Madero 1520 near 16 de Septiembre
Tel: (682) 5-46-88
Clean, cheap, the patio resembles an antique-filled attic. Funky cafe. $

LA CONCHA BEACH RESORT
Carreterra Pichilingue km 5
(5km/3 miles from town)
Tel: (682) 2-65-44
All ocean view rooms; pool, restaurant/bar. $$$

Elegant El Morro

LA POSADA DE ENGELBERT
Avenida Reforma and Playa Sur
(10 minutes along road to airport)
Tel: (682) 2-40-11
Owner Engelbert Humperdinck rarely being here, Mlle Jacqueline presides over beachside suites and a fine restaurant. $$$

PENSION CALIFORNIA
Degollado 209
Tel: (682) 2-28-96
Crowded yard makes it look like a hippy motel without the cars; also has cooking facilities. $

Loreto

HOTEL MISION DE LORETO
Blvd Mateos 1
Tel: (683) 3-00-48
On the *malecón*. Attractive neo-Colonial style with bar, restaurant, pool. $$$

HOTEL OASIS
Blvd Mateos
Tel: (683) 3-02-11
In tropical garden with pool, tennis court, meals included. $$$

HOTEL PLAZA LORETO
Hidalgo 2
Tel: (683) 5-02-80
One block from the mission. Attractive rooms set around a small patio. Bar/restaurant, pool. $$

MOTEL SALVATIERRA
Salvatierra 125
Opposite Pemex station
Tel: (683) 3-00-21
Close to bus station. Clean, plain rooms, bright new blankets on beds. $

SAN MARTIN
Davis and Madero
Tel: (683) 3-00-42
Rock-bottom, dirt-cheap bare rooms. $

STOUFFER PRESIDENTE
Apdo Postal (PO Box) 35
Loreto
Tel: (683) 3-07-00
Self-contained luxury resort, 13km (8 miles) south at Nopolo. $$$

Mexicali

AZTECA DE ORO
Avenida Industria 600
Tel: 57-14-33
Simple, cheap and noisy. $

HOLIDAY INN
Juarez 2220
Tel: (657) 66-13-00
One mile south of town. Swimming pool and restaurant. $$$

HOTEL DEL NORTE
Melgar and Madero
Tel: 52-81-01
Nearest to border. Bar, restaurant, air-conditioning. $

HOTEL PLAZA
Avenida Madero 366
Tel: (62) 52-97-57
Downtown hotel with restaurant and air-conditioning. $

LA LUCERNA
Blvd Benito Juárez 2151
Reservations: PO Box 2300
Calexico, CA 92231
Tel: (656) 6-10-00
Set in attractive grounds. Bar, nightclub, restaurant. $$

Mulegé

CASA HUESPEDES CANNETT
Madero
Tel: (685) 3-02-72
Big white house with balcony. Stone floors, fans, plain but clean. $

HOTEL BAJA HACIENDA
Madero 3
Tel: (685) 3-00-72
Two storys set around an attactive tree-shaded courtyard. Swimming pool, restaurant, bar. $$

HOTEL LAS CASITAS
Madero 50
Tel: (685) 3-00-19
Comfortable rooms around patio with plants, fountains and attractive restaurant. $$

Hotel Las Casitas

HOTEL SERENIDAD
Apdo Postal (PO Box) 9, Mulegé
Tel: (685) 3-011-11
Where the river meets the sea. Comfortable, attractive, bar, restaurant, pool. $$$

HOTEL TERRAZA
Zaragoza
Tel: (685) 3-00-09
Plain rooms, glassed-in terrace bar. $

Rosarito

BAJA VILLAGE MOTEL
Juarez and Via de las Olas 228
Tel: (661) 2-00-50
On main street, adjoining beach. $

CALAFIA
Km 35.5 free road Tijuana–Ensenada
Tel: (661) 2-15-81
Vast, amusingly designed complex of terrace restaurants, bars and bric-à-brac. Pool, 24-hour coffee shop. $$

HOTEL LA FONDA
Km 59 Carretera Tijuana-Ensenada where free and toll highways meet. Reservations: PO Box 430268, San Ysidro, CA 92143 (no phone)
Charming ocean-front hacienda; 4-person studios with kitchens. $$

HOTEL LA MISION
Km 59, adjoins La Fonda (above)
Reservations: PO Box 439060
San Ysidro, CA 92143.
Tel: (661) 2-24-24
Adjoins well-stocked food and liquor store; sports TV nightly. $$

HOTEL PLAZA DEL MAR
PO Box 434520, San Diego, CA 92143
Tel: (668) 5-91-52
Distinctive Mayan pyramid looks over statue-filled garden by ocean, 48km (30 miles) north of Ensenada. Pools, tennis, dining terrace. $$$

LAS ROCAS HOTEL AND SUITES
Km 38.5 free road Tijuana–Ensenada
Tel: (661) 22-21-40
Delightful piano bar and pool in lovely gardens overlooking the ocean. $$$

NEW HOTEL BRISAS DEL MAR
Juarez 22
Tel: (661) 2-25-47
Center of town. Bar and coffee shop. $$$

NEW PORT BAJA HOTEL
PO Box 2776
Chula Vista
CA 92012
Tel: (661) 4-11-88
Situated in Lobster Village south of Rosarito. Pool, tennis, coffee shop. $$

ROSARITO BEACH HOTEL
PO Box 430145
San Diego
CA 92143
Tel: (661) 2-11-06
Legendary resort on highway, with pools, tennis, shopping arcade etc. $$$

San Felipe

EL CORTEZ
Reservations: PO Box 1227,
Calexico, CA 92231
Tel: (011-526) 561-8324
Right by the sea, wide-screen TV. $$

San Ignacio

HOTEL LA POSADA
Avenida Carranza 22
Tel: (685) 13
Spartan but clean. Fans. $

San José del Cabo

EL DELFIN BLANCO
La Playita road near lighthouse
PO Box 147
Tel: (114) 2-11-99
Cabanas and trailer park near beach. $$

FIESTA INN
Paseo Malecón
Tel: (684) 2-07-93
At beach; pool. $$

HOTEL CECI
Zaragoza 22
Tel: 2-00-51
Plain, clean, central, cheap. $

HOTEL COLLI
Hidalgo 10
No phone
Sparse but clean. $

HOTEL PALMILLA
Highway 1, Punta Palmilla
Tel: 2-05-83
Pool, tennis, wedding chapel. $$$

The famous Rosarito Beach

HOTEL POSADA TERRANOVA
Degollado and Zaragoza
Tel: 2-05-34
Restaurant and bar. $

HOWARD JOHNSON'S
Paseo Finisterra off Highway 1
Tel: 2-09-99
Nearly 200 luxury rooms. Distinctive architecture; pool in tropical gardens. $$$

POSADA REAL
Paseo Malecón, on the beach
Tel: 2-07-93
Comfortable resort hotel, pool. $$$

TROPICANA INN
Blvd Mijares 30
Tel: 2-15-80
Pool, fountain, parrot, charming patio restaurant. Free rides to beach. $$

San Quintín

MOTEL CHAVEZ
Apdo Postal (PO Box) 32, San Quintín
Tel: (666) 5-20-05
On highway. Simple, family-type place. $

OLD MILL HOTEL (MOLINO VIEJO)
Reservations: 223 Via de San Ysidro
San Ysidro, CA 92173
Tel: (619) 428-2779
On the eastern shore of the bay. Beautiful, century-old converted mill with a good restaurant and lovely, romantic atmosphere. Fishing trips can be arranged by the management. $$

Santa Rosalia

EL MORRO
On Highway 1
Tel: 2-04-14
Overlooks Gulf of California. Air-conditioning. $

HOTEL BAHIA DE LOS ANGELES
Bottom of Constitución (has no sign)
Small, built around patio. Restaurant next door. $

HOTEL BLANCO Y NEGRO
Serravio 1
Clean and basic. $

HOTEL CENTRAL
Obregón and Calle 4
No phone
Inexpensive and adequate. $

HOTEL DEL REAL
Avenida Manuel F Montoya
Tel: (685) 2-00-68
An attractive wooden building with a terrace. Has a good restaurant and long distance phone. $

HOTEL FRANCIS
Calle 11 de Julio
Tel: 2-08-29
Up the hill near mining office, north end of town. $$

HOTEL OLVERA
Calle Playa 14
Tel: (685) 2-00-57
Near the beach. $

SANTA BARBARA HOTEL
Constitución and Calle 6
Small rooms situated above the corner pharmacy. $

Tecate

HOTEL EL CONQUISTADOR
Blvd Agua Caliente 1777
Tel: 81-79-55
Where the bullfighters stay. $$

HOTEL NELSON
Avenida Revolución 100
Tel: 85-43-02
Simple and inexpensive. $

Tijuana

BEST WESTERN LA MESA INN
Boulevard Díaz Ordaz 50
Tel: 66-81-65-22
Near Agna Caliente Race Track. Pool. $

EL CONQUISTADOR
Boulevard Agua Caliente 1777
Tel: 81-79-55
Pool-side bar evening entertainment. $$

LUCERNA HOTEL
Paseo de los Héroes
Tel: (800) 582-37-62; 84-20-00
Good restaurant; pool, tennis. $$

Lucerna Hotel, a central site

MOTEL PADRE KINO
Boulevard Agua Caliente
Tel: 86-42-08
Basic but pleasant. Pool. $

PALACIO AZTECA
Highway 1, south of Agua Caliente
Tel: 81-81-00
Modern, comfortable, pool, bar. $$

TERRANOVA HOTEL
Boulevard Díaz Ordaz
Tel: 21-03-60
Air-conditioning; color TV in rooms. $$

NIGHTLIFE

There is not a great deal of nightlife in Baja, but the following list includes some of the livelier spots. In addition, many hotels advertise 'Mexican Fiesta' nights with live entertainment.

Tijuana

BABY ROCK
1482 Diego Rivera
Tel: 84-94-38
Disco.

FIESTA AMERICANA HOTEL
4500 Agua Caliente
Tel: 800-343-7825
Disco in hotel.

HEAVEN AND HELL
10501 Paseo de los Héroes
Tel: 84-84-84
Twin dancehalls, closed Sunday, Monday.

OH! LASE CLUB
56 Paseo de los Héroes
Tel: 84-02-67
Disco. Closed Monday to Wednesday.

Ensenada

EL GALEON
Near Sangines and Costero
Tel: 4-04-17
Live music.

KIKI'S
Near Sangines and Costero
Tel: 6-64-60
Live music.

LAS CAZUELAS
Near Sangines and Costero
Tel: 6-1-44
Live music.

Time for tequila

PAPA'S AND BEER
López Mateos and Ruiz
Huge disco.

La Paz

HOTEL PERLA
Obregón 1570
Tel: (682) 20-77-7
Nightclub open until 4am. Closed on Monday.

OKEY LASER
Obregón (one block from Hotel Perla)
Disco music.

San José del Cabo

CACTUS VIDEO
Hotel Stouffer Presidente Los Cabos
On the beach, west of town
Tel: 684-20-21
Disco, weekends only.

Cabo San Lucas

CABO WABO CANTINA
Zaragoza
Tel: 3-11-88
Good dance floor. Concert stage for rock groups.

THE GIGGLING MARLIN
Matamoros, at Marina
Tel: 3-06-06
Lively dance music and gimmicky fun.

WHALE WATCHERS' BAR
Hotel Finisterra
Cabo San Lucas
Tel: (684) 30-00
Mariachi band on terrace.

HEALTH AND EMERGENCIES

No vaccinations are necessary before visiting Baja. Check before leaving home if any are considered advisable.

The upset stomach known as *turista* or Montezuma's revenge is the most common malady suffered by visitors. The best way to avoid this is to stick to *agua mineral* (bottled water) or other bottled drinks and be wary of fruit, vegetables and dairy products. There are doctors available everywhere, of course, and perhaps the easiest way to find them is to ask at the reception desks of the larger hotels. Larger towns have hospitals and pharmacies, but it is sensible to take a first-aid kit. Don't travel without medical insurance cover.

In cases of a real emergency contact the 24-hour service of **Air-Evac International** which operates the Air and Land Ambulance. Emergency: (619) 278-3822. In Mexico tel: 95-800-010-0986.

A specific government department, **Tourist Protection**, exists to help with serious problems such as getting entangled with the police. The officer's name, badge number and car number should be noted and receipts requested for any fines paid. Complaints can then be made to, or help sought from, the Tourist Protection Office in Tijuana (Plaza Patria, Boulevard Diaz Ordaz, tel: 81-9492) or La Paz State Tourism Office (Obregón at 16 de Septiembre, tel: 2-5939). For US citizens, forms concerning police mistreatment are available at the US Consulate in Tijuana (Calle Tapachula, near Agua Caliente, tel: 81-7400) on in Baja Sur from US consular agents located at the Hotel Serenidad in Mulegé, tel: 3-0311. A voluntary organization called the **Binational Emergency Medical Commission** maintains an around-the-clock phone service in Chula Vista (tel: 619/425-5080) offering medical, legal or financial help.

Emergencies
Police tel: **104**
Fire tel: **136**
Red Cross tel: **132**

COMMUNICATIONS AND NEWS

Media
Baja Times: a monthly publication packed with basic tourist information, PO Box 5577, Chula Vista, CA 91912.

Baja Sun: another interesting monthly, PO Box 8530, Chula Vista, CA 91912.

Discover Baja: monthly newsletter, 3065 Clairemont Drive, San Diego, CA 92117.

El Tiempo Los Cabos: helpful bilingual publication.

Telephone / fax
To dial into Mexico, including Baja, from the US, the prefix is 011-52 followed by the specific area code (**66**) or (**67**) for most of the north; (**68**) for the south. Sometimes a third prefix follows before the actual number. Many establishments – particularly hotels – in Baja retain US numbers, making them easier to reach, and some have (800) numbers, which means the call is free. Making telephone calls anywhere in Mexico can be very frustrating – different payphones require different coins – and for long-distance calls it is advisable to look for places signposted *Larga Distancia* (Long Distance), of which there is at least one in any sizeable community. As in other countries, hotels tend to add a hefty surcharge for calls made through the switchboard but the service can be useful. And as commercial fax places are rare, hotels are sometimes the only places from which faxes can be sent.

Make your calls here

LANGUAGE

Outside the main tourist areas most people speak very little English, so it is advisable to take a good Spanish phrase book with you. Listed below are a few useful expressions.

Buenos días	Good morning
Buenos tardes	Good afternoon
Buenos noches	Good night
Por favor	Please
Gracias	Thank you
Si	Yes
No	No
¿Habla Inglés?	Do you speak English
No entiendo	I don't understand
¿Donde está…?	Where is…?

¿Cuanto se tarda en llegar?	
	How long does it take to get there?
¿Cuantos kilometros hay…?	
	How many kilometers/ how far is it?
¿Cuanto es? Cuanto vale?	
	How much is…?
el aeropuerto	the airport
la estación	the station
el autobus	the bus
el avion	the plane
el tren	the train
el boleto/el billete	the ticket
una habitación/un cuarto	
	a room
…con baño	…with bath
la gasolinera	petrol station
Lleno, por favor	Full, please (as for petrol)
el aceite	oil
el agua	water
el hielo	ice
la llave	the key
caro	expensive
barato/económico	cheap

USEFUL INFORMATION

Tours

Whale-watching

Baja Expeditions 2625 Garnet Avenue, San Diego, CA 92109. Tel: (619) 581-3311. Whale watching, kayaking, sailing, scuba diving.

Baja Discovery PO Box 152527, San Diego, CA 92115 Tel: (619) 262-0700. Four- to eight-day whale-watching trips (January to March, and October); other adventure tours in winter.

Snorkeling and Diving

Baja Diving Service Independencia 107 La Paz. Tel: 2-27-44. Sightseeing, diving, snorkeling, etc.

Mulegé Divers (Miguel and Claudia) Madero 45, tel: 3-01-34. Trips to the islands, Punta Concepción. Even the inexperienced can explore the Sea of Córtez with mask, fins and snorkel

Tourcabos Plaza Los Cabos, San José del Cabos, tel: (684) 2-09-82. Sunset cruises, snorkeling or diving tours, whale-watching, fossil beds, etc.

Chubasco's Blvd Marina 22, tel: (684) 3-04-04. Tours to lighthouse, and to mountain village of La Candelaria.

El Delfín Blanco PO Box 147, San José del Cabo, tel: (114) 2-11-99.

Other tours

Pescadores de Mulegé, Fishing fleet located next to Hotel Serenidad. Information from the US, tel: (310) 865-4490.

Baja California Tours, 6986 La Jolla Blvd, La Jolla, CA 92037, tel: (619) 454-7166. Three-day motor coach tours to Rosarito Beach, Ensenada or San Felipe.

Touring Exchange, PO Box 265, Port Townsend, WA 98368, tel: (206) 385-0667. Owner Bonnie Wong conducts 14-day bicycle tours of Baja.

Cruz Arce, Suarez and Agua Dulce, Loreto, tel: (683) 5-02-03. Indian cave paintings trip.

Sports

Fishing, of course, is what has drawn most visitors to Baja for years, although in all coastal resorts windsurfing and water skiing are catching up fast. A license to fish in Mexican waters is required, especially for boats carrying fishing tackle, in which case everybody aboard must have a license bearing his or her name. Licenses, valid for the week, month or year, are obtainable from the Mexican Dept of Fisheries, 2550 5th Avenue, Suite 101, San Diego, CA 92103, tel: (619) 233-6956.

Ferries

Santa Rosalia to Guaymas

Ferries from Santa Rosalia leave late at night on Sunday, Tuesday and Thursday, arriving at approximately 7am. The return trip from Guaymas starts around 10am (tel: 852/00-13)

The marina at Loreto

Heavenly horizon

The mainland to La Paz

Sematur operates boats to and from Mazatlán each afternoon, arriving on the other side of the gulf the following morning. Cabins are advisable; they are relatively inexpensive. Six days a week there are boats to and from Topolobampo, a trip that takes about nine hours (tel: 91-800-696-96).

USEFUL ADDRESSES

Baja Information
7860 Mission Center Court No 2
San Diego
CA 92108
Tel: (800) 225-2786 from the US; (800) 522-1516 from California.

Baja State Tourism US Office
PO Box 2448
Chula Vista
CA 91912

Tijuana Chamber of Commerce
Revolución and Calle 1
Tel: (66) 85-84-72

Tourist offices

Tijuana Tourist Information Office
Edificio Paseo Héroes 2
Paseo de los Héroes
Tel: 84-05-37

Tourist Information Office
Avenida López Mateos 1306 and Avenida Blancante 128
Tel: 8-24-11

Rosarito
State Tourist Office
Blvd Juárez 100
Tel: (661) 2-02-00

Ensenada
State Tourist Commission
Avenida López Mateos 1305
Tel: (667) 6-22-22

San Quintín
State Tourist Office
Km 192, Ensenada–San Quintín Highway
Tel: (666) 5-23-76

San Felipe
Tourist Office, El Marino
Avenida Mar de Cortez and Calz Chetumal
Tel: 7-11-83

FURTHER READING

Insight Guides: Mexico (APA Publications, 1994)

Baja California & Its Missions by Tomás Robertson (La Siesta Press, Glendale, 1978)

Baja California (Automobile Club of Southern California, 1993)

Black Robes in Lower California by Peter Masten Dunne (University of California Press, 1952)

Juan Maria de Salvatierra: Selected Letters about Lower California (Dawsons Book Shop, Los Angeles, 1971)

The History of Lower California by Don Francisco Javier Clavigera (Manessier Publishing Co, Riverside, 1971)

Index

T, U, V, W

ACKNOWLEDGMENTS

Photography Marcus Wilson Smith

Production Editor Mohammed Dar
Handwriting V.Barl
Cover Design Klaus Geisler
Cartography Lovell Johns

NOTES

INSIGHT GUIDES

COLORSET NUMBERS

INSIGHT *pocket* GUIDES

United States: **Houghton Mifflin Company, Boston MA 02108**
Tel: (800) 2253362 Fax: (800) 4589501

Canada: **Thomas Allen & Son, 390 Steelcase Road East**
Markham, Ontario L3R 1G2
Tel: (416) 4759126 Fax: (416) 4756747

Great Britain: **GeoCenter UK, Hampshire RG22 4BJ**
Tel: (256) 817987 Fax: (256) 817988

Worldwide: **Höfer Communications Singapore 2262**
Tel: (65) 8612755 Fax: (65) 8616438

66 I was first drawn to the Insight Guides by the excellent "Nepal" volume. I can think of no book which so effectively captures the essence of a country. Out of these pages leaped the Nepal I know – the captivating charm of a people and their culture. I've since discovered and enjoyed the entire Insight Guide Series. Each volume deals with a country or city in the same sensitive depth, which is nowhere more evident than in the superb photography. **99**

Sir Edmund Hillary